THE GREATEST LAKE

THE GREATEST LAKE

Stories from Lake Superior's North Shore

CONOR MIHELL

DUNDURN
TORONTO

Editor: Shannon Whibbs
Design: Jesse Hooper
Printer: Webcom

Library and Archives Canada Cataloguing in Publication

Mihell, Conor
          The greatest lake : stories from Lake Superior's north shore / Conor Mihell.

Includes bibliographical references and index.
Issued also in electronic formats.
ISBN 978-1-4597-0246-2

          1. Superior, Lake--History. 2. Superior, Lake, Region--Anecdotes. 3. Superior, Lake, Region--Biography.
I. Title.

FC3095.S86M55 2012   971.3'12   C2012-900135-X

1   2   3   4   5   16   15   14   13   12

We acknowledge the support of the **Canada Council for the Arts** and the **Ontario Arts Council** for our publishing program. We also acknowledge the financial support of the **Government of Canada** through the **Canada Book Fund** and **Livres Canada Books**, and the **Government of Ontario** through the **Ontario Book Publishing Tax Credit** and the **Ontario Media Development Corporation**.

Care has been taken to trace the ownership of copyright material used in this book. The author and the publisher welcome any information enabling them to rectify any references or credits in subsequent editions.
                                                                                                      J. Kirk Howard, President

Printed and bound in Canada.
www.dundurn.com

Front cover images: (Top row, l–r) Sunset from Otter Island, Pukaskwa National Park; Light beacon at the mouth of the Michipicoten River in an October gale; Waves on rock, Slate Islands Provincial Park; The Canadian Coast Guard's Parisienne Island Lighthouse, west of Sault Ste. Marie.
(Bottom) Sea-kayaking in rough water near Pic Island, Neys Provincial Park. Photo by Kim Mihell.
Back cover image: Sunset at Michipicoten Bay.

Dundurn	Gazelle Book Services Limited	Dundurn
3 Church Street, Suite 500	White Cross Mills	2250 Military Road
Toronto, Ontario, Canada	High Town, Lancaster, England	Tonawanda, NY
M5E 1M2	LA1 4XS	U.S.A. 14150

In memory of T.J. O'Connor (1915–2010),
who knew no greater pleasure than sharing his love for Lake Superior with others

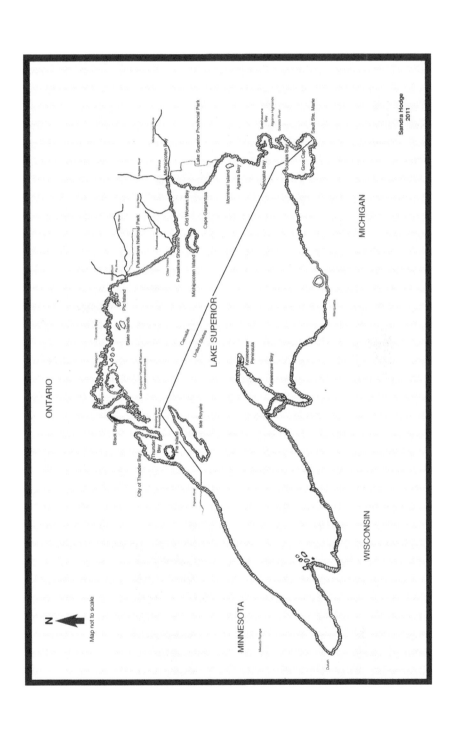

N

Map not to scale

ONTARIO

MINNESOTA

WISCONSIN

MICHIGAN

LAKE SUPERIOR

Canada
United States

Sandra Hodge
2011

City of Thunder Bay

Black Bay

Thunder
Bay

Pie Island

Isle Royale

Slate Islands

Pic Island

Pukaskwa National Park

Pukaskwa Shoreline

Michipicoten Island

Old Woman Bay

Cape Gargantua

Montreal Island

Agawa Bay

Lake Superior Provincial Park

Michipicoten Bay

Batchawana Bay

Algoma Highlands

Gros Cap

Sault Ste. Marie

Keweenaw
Peninsula

Keweenaw Bay

Duluth

CONTENTS

INTRODUCTION
Searching for Inchcape Rock

Geologists would call the refrigerator-sized chunk of sandstone resting in two metres of water at the mouth of the St. Marys River in Lake Superior's east end an "erratic." By all definitions, the rock shouldn't be there. Surrounded by miles of sandy bottom and buttressed to the north by the stalwart granite monolith of Gros Cap, this block of relatively young, soft, sedimentary stone is evidence of a former, distant seabed. It would have been deposited at random by the retreating glacier at the end of the last ice age, ten-thousand-odd years ago.

Erratic also described our chances of finding this misplaced rock, which my grandfather named Inchcape after the feared Scottish shoal that ripped open the hulls of many a passing ship. The shoal was immortalized by an 1820 poem by Robert Southey, essential reading for grade-schoolers like my grandfather in the 1920s. However, Grandpa's Inchcape Rock was more benign. When I was a kid, about once a summer we'd stumble upon it on an afternoon outing in his seventeen-foot sailboat. Then we'd hastily come about and toss overboard a brick-anchored Javex bottle float he always carried in the sailboat expressly for the purpose of marking Inchcape Rock, just in case we saw it.

The discovery sparked much excitement. The next day, we'd pile back into the sailboat with a full complement of flippers, masks, and snorkels, fire up the archaic two-horsepower motor if the wind wasn't blowing, and head offshore at a snail's pace in a cloud of blue exhaust. We'd then spend a few hours revelling in a swimming hole my grandfather deemed to be Lake Superior's finest. While the kids dove off the boat and played King of the Castle on the rock, Grandpa would sip Scotch whisky mixed with icy-cold lake water brought up from the bottom by a willing swimmer. Then he'd engage in an exercise of geometry known to sailors as "range-finding," attempting to line up features on shore to assist in future missions in search of Inchcape Rock. Needless to say, these calculations achieved varying degrees of success; Inchcape's exact whereabouts could never be pinpointed.

T.J. O'Connor at the tiller of the Pokey II, *his seventeen-foot sailboat, on Lake Superior at the mouth of the St. Marys River. O'Connor sailed these shallow waters well into his eighties, always on the lookout for the infamous Inchcape Rock, a sedimentary monolith deposited by glaciers in the otherwise sandy bay that he named after a famous 1820 poem by Robert Southey.*

Inevitably — and usually within the next few days — gale-force winds would blow out of the northwest and the Javex bottle would drag anchor and disappear, rendering the day or two we spent swimming from the sailboat at Inchcape Rock but a happy memory. This elusiveness gave the place a mystical quality; its discovery marked the fleeting climax of summer. The next year we'd chance upon it again, and the tradition continued.

I blame my grandfather for the wanderlust that has had me piloting small, paddle-powered boats across gulfs of open water in search of other Inchcape Rocks up and down Lake Superior's north shore. He's the one who introduced me to the place and shared with me a fascination for the world's largest expanse of freshwater. My grandparents, Mae and T.J. O'Connor, purchased a cottage lot on Sunnyside Beach in 1954. At the time, the five-kilometre-long sweep of sand located barely twenty-five kilometres west of downtown Sault Ste. Marie was considered to be very remote, accessible by rutted, sandy roads through a thick, swampy forest.

T.J. wasted no time in putting up a modest cottage where his family spent entire summers while he made the epic commute to and from "town" where he owned an electrical shop. The camp was pieced together with odds and ends, most of which were acquired for free or at deep five-finger discounts. A design statement it wasn't — the teal-green, cedar-sided camp featured crimson trim, and, in the living room, a pink asbestos tile floor. Meals were concocted on a wood-burning stove, adding a degree of coziness to summer evenings. Boats came and went — a barge-like houseboat he built over the course of a winter in the basement of his Sault Ste. Marie home, a water-ski boat, and a string of sailboats, one of which was known as the *Sunnyside Up* — and so did the children.

Among the handful of early Sunnyside Beach cottagers, the O'Connors were best known for T.J.'s swimming expeditions and Mae's affinity for happy hour, where she was always the life of the party. The houseboat was capable of carrying dozens of youths for afternoon swims in the deep-water pool surrounding infamous Inchcape Rock. The houseboat's cabin-top diving board was a big hit, especially amongst the teenage boys who would constantly try to one-up each other's dives, much to T.J.'s enjoyment. When T.J. returned — always in time for five o'clock happy hour — Mae would chastise him for neglecting to head-count his troops before setting off on the water and returning for the day. "What if you left one swimming way out there?" she'd ask. "Then what would we do?" But best we can tell, no kids were ever forgotten at Inchcape Rock.

I grew up in the children's paradise that was Sunnyside Beach. The beach's sand was just the right texture and consistency for castle-building and its water was warm and shallow. The bay was so shallow, in fact, that each summer a few adventurous souls would walk to Seagull Island, a tiny, mop-topped sandbank three kilometres offshore, with the water never cresting their necks. Evenings were spent around massive bonfires whose flames punctuated the night sky and made for a new outdoor sport: crafting airplanes from newspaper and seeing whose jet could survive the most flights through the pyre. Offshore, the Gros Cap lighthouse — once an old ship anchored atop the dangerous shoals marking the mouth of the St. Marys River — would flicker in the darkness, and the lights from the odd freighter plying the open water would break the horizon.

Slowly, the community at Sunnyside Beach matured. By the time I entered the picture, T.J. and Mae had sold their house in town and lived year-round in the recently remodelled cottage. Wetlands were filled and a new road

The author's first boat, a twelve-foot aluminum rowboat painted with the dregs of Grandpa T.J.'s most recent project — once crimson red, later forest green. A fresh coat of paint never made it less leaky.

— first gravel, then paved — was punched through the old swamp in behind the beach, opening up more cottage lots. Because the road fell within city limits, streetlights were installed — much to the chagrin of some cottagers. My grandpa always said it was the streetlights that marked the beach's transition from seasonal getaway to bedroom community in the 1980s.

When I was a teenager, T.J. taught me how to take care of the place. The annual task of cutting down a tree was my favourite project. Every spring, my grandma would joke that the trees shuddered every time my grandfather went outside. She swore that the papery bark of the birches fluttered and the maple leaves quivered when T.J. gazed their way, sizing them up for harvest. Despite my grandma's pleas to leave the trees be, nearly each summer he picked out a maple with a crooked trunk or a dead-topped birch he was convinced would fall on the cottage roof. The son of a northern Ontario lumberjack, T.J. relished unearthing his antiquated chain- and swede-saws, blunt-edged axes, and one-ton come-along, and calling me out to assist with some good old-fashioned logging.

His unique, labour-intensive approach always evolved into summer-long projects. Growing up during the Depression, T.J. wanted to be a dentist. Though he never achieved these aspirations, his approach to forestry bore striking similarities to removing a tooth. When he became too old to do it himself, in his late eighties, he'd first have a professional lop off the top of the tree. Then he would employ me to dig out the roots, while he observed from a lawnchair, occasionally blasting the roots with water from a hose to remove dirt. Next I'd cut the roots, a dangerous, shot-in-the-dark, sparky procedure. Finally, we'd pull down the tree with a come-along, section the trunk, and fill in the cavity left by the roots. Then came the jobs of splitting and stacking. It felt satisfying to burn the wood I'd cut a summer or two before while we watched *Hockey Night in Canada* in the winter.

I dreamed of buying my grandparents' camp sometime in the future. I think the notion would've pleased my grandfather to no end. Ironically, though, it was his sense of curiosity and love of Lake Superior that set me on journeys of my own. I remember sitting on the breakwall at the edge of the beach and watching countless sunsets with T.J. in all seasons. I believed him when he'd say, "For now, this as close as we'll get to heaven."

And then I sea-kayaked the coastline of Lake Superior Provincial Park and saw the sun set over the volcanic islands of Tugboat Channel, near

Gargantua; I camped on the beaches of Pukaskwa National Park and watched a fiery ball extinguished by an open, watery horizon that might as well have been the ocean; and I saw the smoke of distant forest fires turn the sun into molten copper while paddling around the Slate Islands. Meanwhile, monster homes of the privileged started lining the shore of Sunnyside Beach, and it was no longer Grandpa T.J.'s trees that shuddered. The sound of excavators and nailing guns replaced the laughter of children. While my grandparents wondered where the Sunnyside of old had gone, I set off in search of a new Inchcape Rock.

I thought about Grandpa T.J. a lot during the eight months I spent in Vancouver, where I studied journalism at the University of British Columbia. I'd lived away from home before — including the better part of four years in southern Ontario while completing my undergraduate degree — but never had I been so far removed from Lake Superior. When I moved away, I thought it would be easy. I imagined falling in love with the Pacific coast and Rocky Mountains, sea-kayaking and backcountry skiing year-round. But come spring, as my first year of graduate school came to an end, all I wanted to do was go home.

As soon as my classes ended in April, I drove for four days over the mountains and across the Prairies, my little old pickup truck beleaguered by the weight of all my possessions. When I grew road-weary, I shuffled my gear in the back and slept in abandoned roadside parks and behind service stations, bundled in my goose-down sleeping bag to ward off the late-winter chill. When I hit Thunder Bay, I knew I was getting close. I bought food and filled my campstove with fuel. I stopped at the Terry Fox Lookout east of the Lakehead to gaze out at the Sleeping Giant, whose cliffs towered above the lake. Finally, I pulled over at Rossport, packed and launched my sea kayak into water that only days before had been ice, and set off. I envisioned myself running into Lake Superior's open arms and receiving a hero's welcome, like a wayward son come home.

Instead, I felt cold spray on my face and spent three days crashing through newly formed morning ice and bucking headwinds, huddling close to the campfire at night and paddling a maniac course to Swede Island, where I knew a hidden sauna and long-abandoned cabin awaited. I realized that the lake couldn't care less that I was back, but every time I scooped a cup of its icy water and gulped its sweet goodness I smiled at the knowledge that I was home.

It upset my grandfather that I never went back to Vancouver to finish the master's degree program I'd started. But at the same time I think he understood the feelings that I had. I too was hopelessly in love with a magical place. My Inchcape Rock rested beyond the horizon of Sunnyside Beach, along the wild north shore of the greatest lake.

CHAPTER 1

The Keeper of the Trowbridge Island Light

I first heard about Trowbridge Island from Darrell Makin, a sea kayaker and outdoor recreation instructor at Lakehead University in Thunder Bay, in 2005. He told me about an island off the tip of the Sibley Peninsula and the bizarre world an older, retired woman had created there. Maureen Robertson rented the lighthouse buildings on Trowbridge Island from the Canadian Coast Guard, and had decorated the place with whimsical treasures she found at yard sales and thrift shops and hauled to her island hermitage each year by helicopter. "Every room in the house has a rotary telephone," Makin told me, despite the fact there is no telephone service to the island. "There's a signed picture of Ronald Reagan, a post office and a roomful of stuffed dolls. You've got to go there — she loves kayakers."

For several years, the notes Makin made on my chart of northwestern Lake Superior faded to obscurity while I spent my summers paddling the waters of the eastern half of the lake, closer to Wawa and Sault Ste. Marie. Then, in 2008, I guided a week-long trip from the Minnesota-Ontario border at Pigeon River to the village of Silver Islet at the tip of the Sibley Peninsula, a once-bustling nineteenth-century mining shantytown turned quaint cottage community.

The route is made up of a series of open-water crossings between a series of offshore islands. On a calm July morning, we awoke at sunrise and paddled nervously across the ten-kilometre gap separating Pie Island and Thunder Cape, a channel that's plied by freighters heading to and from the port in Thunder Bay. Thunder Cape is the site of a remote bird observatory, accessible only by water or a rough, twelve-kilometre-long trail. Ornithologists Maureen and John Woodcock gave us a friendly tour of the facility. Upon leaving, I remembered Trowbridge. "Oh, you really should go," said Maureen. "And bring these cookies and grapefruit for Maureen [Robertson]. She lives out there all alone all summer long and always appreciates fresh food. You're going to love her."

Although we were exhausted from the early-morning crossing, we had little else to do for the day and decided to venture out to tiny Trowbridge Island.

The visit was the highlight of the trip. Robertson took us through the duplex lighthouse keepers' residences and wowed us with her odd tastes for decorating. She posed for pictures, told us stories of the dozen-odd summers she'd spent on Trowbridge, and gave us the keys to the light tower and encouraged us to enjoy the view from the top. My group was so enamoured with Robertson's fairytale-like place that I had to pry them away. When I left, I promised Robertson that I would come again.

My visit to Trowbridge Island in 2010 was equal parts serendipitous and bittersweet. Robertson had decided that this would be her last summer on the island, and, largely by chance, I paddled out for an overnight visit on an assignment for Cottage Life *magazine merely a week before she left the place for good. My mind raced with interview questions, but besides the nuts and bolts of when and how she began "cottaging" on a remote island on Lake Superior, mostly I wanted to know why she was drawn to the solitude. Our extended conversations, interrupted only by the sounds of wind chimes and waves on the lake, told of a seventy-six-year-old woman kept young by a life on Lake Superior.*

Gypsy Moth Island is absent from even the most detailed maps of Lake Superior. But the place exists in the mind of Maureen Robertson, its last resident, and in the imagination of the few who were lucky enough to visit her there. For fourteen years, Robertson spent her springs, summers, and falls alone on this rockbound, nine-acre island that's located twenty-five kilometres as the seagull flies from her home in Thunder Bay, Ontario. On nautical charts, Robertson's island is labelled Trowbridge, with the subscript *Fl5s114Ft16M*. For years, Trowbridge's raison d'être was its lighthouse, which flashes once every five seconds, stands 114 feet above the high water mark, and is visible for sixteen nautical miles. But when Robertson moved in, the enchanted island she came to know as Gypsy Moth became much more.

In March or April — in some years before the ice broke up between the thousand-foot cliffs of the Sibley Peninsula and the commercial shipping channel leading to and from the Lakehead — Robertson would charter a helicopter to Trowbridge. It's only a six-minute flight from the Thunder Bay airport to the island's Canadian Coast Guard–maintained helipad. Upon landing, she unloaded crates of Chef Boyardee and other non-perishable supplies, convinced the pilot that she'd survive the season alone — without electricity, running water, or a telephone — and settled in for another stint at the lighthouse she rented from the federal government.

On a sunny July day, the seventy-six-year-old Robertson shows me around the old two-storey semi-detached lighthouse keepers' residences where she's lived for up to six months of the year since 1997. She's decorated each of the building's eight rooms thematically with whimsical yard-sale and thrift-store treasures. On the first floor, there's a re-created post office, complete with a red enamelled, breadbox-style mailbox. Tacked to the walls are old photographs of various heads of state — Jean Chrétien, Pierre Trudeau, and a signed portrait of Ronald Reagan. "A lot of Americans ask why I have a picture of *him*," says Robertson. "But I like him. I don't care about politics; he was the only one who sent me an autographed picture."

Above Chrétien and Reagan are the words GYPSY MOTH. "I didn't like the name 'Trowbridge' so I decided to change it to Gypsy Moth [after de Havilland's 1920s-era biplane]," says Robertson. "There was one crotchety guy at the Coast Guard who said, 'you can't do that.' I just laughed and told him the sign at the post office was already up and what was he going to do about it?"

Her favourite space in the house is an upstairs bedroom dedicated to the Royal Canadian Mounted Police, complete with a pair of wooden snowshoes, the bed covered with faux (leopard) and real (beaver) fur blankets and the walls covered with various Norman Rockwell–style prints of Mounties, all inspired by an encounter she had as a child growing up in the northern Ontario railway town of Mobert. "The Mountie got off the train and he was six-foot-something and so handsome," she recalls. "For us girls it was like we'd just seen a Greek god. Ever since I've always thought the Mounties were out of this world." Early in the spring, when sunshine and a small kerosene heater are her only source of warmth, Robertson will sit and read by the window of the RCMP room.

A children's room is filled with thirty-eight stuffed Teletubby dolls; another bedroom has a collage of 1920s-vintage *Vogue* magazine covers on the walls; and the downstairs kitchen is inspired by a vacation she took to Egypt. Throughout the place she's turned old ladders into towel racks and bricks and boards into bookshelves; nearly every room in the house has an old rotary telephone, despite the island's lack of phone service.

Among Robertson's whimsically decorated rooms is a re-created post office, complete with an autographed photograph of former United States president Ronald Reagan.

"When I got it, nobody had been in here in years," says Robertson. "The front door wouldn't even shut." Her first order of duty was painting the walls with the dregs of fifty-five discarded gallon-sized cans of paint, courtesy of the Sears store in Thunder Bay. Then it took her four years to decorate, hauling things in piece by piece by helicopter and salvaging what she could find on the island. "It was like, here's a house, now do whatever you like with it," she says. "So I just went crazy." She admits that most of her visitors think she's somewhat peculiar — if only for her kitschy decor. "If they're going to think I'm eccentric," she concedes, "then I'm going to live up to it."

Robertson hasn't restricted her curious interior designs to Trowbridge. She tells me that each of the three bedrooms of her modest mobile home in Thunder Bay have unique design inspirations. Her master bedroom is "all done up in purple and gold lamé," and the spare bedrooms have African and dollhouse themes.

By mid-afternoon, the wind picks up out of the southwest, whipping the wind chimes on the front verandah, where we sit and chat over a pot of inky tea. The setting is so surreal, the house friendly, happy, and incongruous with its rugged surroundings. My thoughts become lost in the dreamlike sights and sounds of this unlikely place, dulling my senses and causing me to fade in and out of our conversation. It's hard to believe that once upon a time, lighthouse keepers had one of the most perilous and lonely jobs around. Robertson says she hoped "her" island would be different. "I always wanted it to be surprising," she says, "to feel like you just stumbled upon this fairytale place in the middle of nowhere."

Mission accomplished, I'd say.

Viewed from Silver Islet, the quaint cottage community on Lake Superior at the end of Highway 587, an hour's drive east of Thunder Bay, Trowbridge can be distinguished from a handful of ship-shaped islands only by the break in its treeline caused by the lighthouse, which from a distance resembles a sailboat's mast. It's also the farthest offshore, about three kilometres from the mainland at its closest point, marking the northern edge of open water plied by thousand-foot freighters. The nearest land to the south is Isle Royale, Lake Superior's largest island and a U.S. national park that belongs to the state of Michigan, which barely registers on the horizon. Like most of Superior's north shore, the expanse of perpetually cold water and rugged coastline are intimi-dating and foreboding. The towering sandstone cliffs of the Sibley Peninsula, which take on the shape of a prostrate giant, are the tallest in Ontario. The shores of Trowbridge and its neighbouring islands are comprised of smaller, but equally inhospitable cliffs and jagged boulders the shape of bar fridges and panel vans.

Trowbridge is one of several light stations on western Lake Superior, established in a time when increasing commercial shipping, sketchy charts, and primitive piloting technology made aids to navigation essential. The lake's first light was installed in 1867 on isolated, sliver-shaped Talbot Island, located one hundred kilometres east of Thunder Bay. In its six years of operation, three keepers of the so-called "Lighthouse of Doom" died. The first perished in a boating accident while trying to escape the island before winter. Thomas Lamphier, the second keeper, planned to overwinter at Talbot with his wife. But when Lamphier died suddenly, his wife was forced to tend his frozen corpse for months. She is said to have been discovered in a state of madness come spring, her once-black hair a ghostly white. After the third lightkeeper disap-peared without a trace in another late-season boating mishap, the Canadian government abandoned the Talbot light. The foundation of the tower is barely visible today, buried amidst brambles atop a crumbling cliff.

The three-hundred-metre-tall sedimentary cliffs of the Sleeping Giant dwarf Trowbridge Island, where a beacon has marked the north edge of the shipping channel leading into Thunder Bay since 1924.

By 1877, lights were established at Porphyry, Lamb, and Battle islands, about forty-five, eighty, and 130 kilometres east of the Lakehead, respectively. At the time, most commercial boat traffic on the lake followed the inshore route amidst the hundreds of islands of what's now the Lake Superior National Marine Conservation Area. Though automated, all three lights remain active today, guiding the course of pleasure boaters in the area. The Trowbridge light was erected in 1924, nearly two decades after a November storm wrecked the steamer *Theano*, a 255-foot steel ocean-going freighter, on its east shore. Before Global Positioning Systems practically rendered careful, observation-based navigation from the wheelhouse obsolete, Trowbridge's beacon was critical in guiding mariners along the deepwater channel to Thunder Bay. All told, the flash of sixteen beacons still light up the night in Lake Superior's Canadian waters today.

At the turn of the twentieth century, lighthouse keepers often had to find their own way to and from some of the most isolated places on the Great Lakes. In 1916, it took William Sherlock, the keeper of a light on north-eastern Lake Superior's Michipicoten Island, more than a week to cross forty-five kilometres of open water in an unrelenting December storm in an eighteen-foot sailboat. George Johnston, the keeper of the Great Lakes' most isolated lighthouse on tiny Caribou Island, located over one hundred kilometres from the mainland, endured a similarly harrowing eight-day epic in late 1919. Sherlock's luck ran out when he went missing for good at the end of the 1917 season; unfazed, his wife took over his responsibilities on Michipicoten Island, a post she held until 1925.

The responsibilities of early lighthouse keepers included tending the whale oil- or kerosene-fuelled lantern, ensuring the steam-powered foghorn was primed and ready to be activated, recording weather observations, and ensuring associated pieces of machinery were in working order. Pay was hardly commensurate with the long hours of lonely, stressful work. In 1922, for instance, Mary Sherlock took home a paltry annual salary of only $900.

Diesel electric generators and, in a few less remote lighthouses, high-voltage cables from the mainland, made the task of keeping the light lit less onerous in later years. But the isolation still made it a difficult job: According to Great Lakes lighthouse historian Larry Wright, a bitter feud developed between two keepers stationed at the Gros Cap Crib light at the mouth of the St. Marys River, west of Sault Ste. Marie, in the 1970s; and the last keeper of

Porphyry Island was reportedly relieved of his duties after he broadcast one too many panicked marine radio messages that UFOs were attempting to land on the island's helipad.

Eventually, improved electronics and navigation instruments on ships in the 1980s enabled the "destaffing" of Great Lakes lighthouses, says Canadian Coast Guard officer Ron Walker, who has been working in the industry for over twenty years. Orton and Ruth Rumley, the last keepers of the Trowbridge light, left their job in 1989. The last lighthouse to be automated on the Great Lakes was at Michipicoten Harbour, near the town of Wawa, in 1990.

The musty, rotting, and lichen-encrusted remains of this forgotten occupation — buildings, boathouses, sheds, and elaborate poured concrete walkways and piers — are still standing at most Lake Superior lighthouses. Typically, two lightkeepers shared shift work at a site for the duration of the shipping season from March until December, hence the duplex residence at Trowbridge Island. Other light stations had detached residences for each family. Architecture was decidedly consistent from one place to the next: The keepers' old two-storey house and more modern bungalow at Otter Island, in present-day Pukaskwa National Park, are a facsimile of those at Slate Islands, offshore from the town of Terrace Bay. Similarly, the semi-detached house at Battle Island is a mirror image to that at Trowbridge.

After the lights were automated, Walker says a few former keepers and their families struck agreements with the Coast Guard to cottage at Lake Superior lighthouses. A handful of lights are still occupied under such arrangements, including the Slate Island lighthouse on the south side of Mortimer Island, offshore of Terrace Bay, and the Battle Island light near Rossport. Walker says Maureen Robertson is unique, however, in that she had no previous association with the Coast Guard or Trowbridge Island.

Robertson had all but finished decorating her island retreat when, in May 2010, the federal government listed twelve "surplus lighthouses" on Lake Superior, including Trowbridge Island, as a part of the newly created Heritage Lighthouses Protection Act. The Parks Canada–administered program invites Canadian citizens to petition government "to conserve and protect" heritage lighthouses from a small list of candidate sites, such as the iconic navigational aid at Peggy's Cove, Nova Scotia. The bulk of Canadian beacons — 986 of them to be exact — have been deemed "surplus," meaning that they could "be replaced with simpler structures whose operation and maintenance would be more cost-effective," or extinguished permanently. Under the act, Fisheries and Oceans Canada has the option to offload these lights to willing members of the public to do with them as they please.

Parks Canada solicited nominations from the public not-for-profit agencies for the preservation of lighthouses "considered to possess significant heritage values" until the spring of 2012. Petitioners were required to collect the signatures of at least twenty-five Canadians; regulations state that properties must be "properly maintained" and any modifications to structures must be first approved by a heritage committee. While responding to calls from history buffs to protect iconic lighthouses in popular tourist destinations like Peggy's Cove, Nova Scotia, the Heritage Lighthouses Protection Act has been criticized for compromising the future of remote lighthouses that escape the public eye. It leaves "the door open to the lighthouses' abandonment and demolition by neglect," says Carolyn Quinn, a spokesperson for the Heritage Canada Foundation, an Ottawa-based, not-for-profit organization. In the case of Lake Superior, the new legislation could signal the end of an era.

On a calm morning, my lightweight, resilient, plastic sea kayak seems like the ideal vessel to visit Trowbridge Island. It's easier to get there by powerboat, but the island's exposed concrete pier makes landing a challenge, and the derrick that lifted boats from Superior's destructive grasp now stands rusty and derelict. When I arrived at Silver Islet in a foggy twilight the night before, the lake appeared malevolent and discontent. The bleakness of the scene was intimidating. But all seems well on this sunny morning, and it takes me about two hours to island-hop from the public boat launch at the end of Highway 587 to Trowbridge. When I get there, I pull ashore on a patch of ankle-twisting rocks that's partially sheltered from the vast sweep of open water to the south by a rock spire. After scaling a small cliff and negotiating tangled clumps of dwarf birch, I climb atop the helicopter-landing pad. Pausing to catch my breath, I glimpse a partially nude sunbather on the front porch of the white-and-red keepers' residences. A friend warned me of this. My hollered-out greeting is received with a shriek.

"Don't go anywhere!" Maureen Robertson says as she scampers behind the house. "I just need to put some clothes on. I'll be back in a minute."

Robertson emerges wearing one-piece blue canvas coveralls emblazoned with Royal Air Force crests, various lapel pins, and five prominent stars embroidered above the chest pocket. She's fit and tanned, with a shock of white hair, a wide smile, and deep crow's feet radiating from her friendly eyes. She apologizes for our awkward first encounter — "there's no way you want to see a naked old lady at this time in the morning" — and invites me into the south side of the duplex. We linger in the fuchsia-walled living room while Robertson launches into the story of the "cute little pilot" who began her tenure at Lake Superior lighthouses. It's hard not to be distracted by the lime-green sofa, matching chair, and 1980s-vintage portrait of her four sons on the table by the window. The floor sags disconcertingly beneath a royal blue carpet.

When she was still working as a clerk at a health clinic in Thunder Bay, Robertson would vacation in the boreal forest and lakes northeast of the city, flying to outpost fishing and hunting camps for a week or so of alone time "in the bush." It was something she'd been doing since she roamed the wilds of northern Ontario as a child with her father, a prospector, teacher, and railroad station manager. One year, a young float-plane pilot picked her up at a fly-in camp and invited her to "go for a bit of a ride." No arm-twisting was necessary. "I just love airplanes," says Robertson, "so I said sure."

They flew over the waters of northwestern Lake Superior, which are speckled with hundreds of islands in a manner that's not unlike Georgian Bay — except that the topography is more dramatic and the islands are covered with a mop-topped mix of black spruce, balsam fir, and birch. At the tip of the boot-shaped Black Bay Peninsula, Robertson spotted the lighthouse and keepers' residences on Porphyry Island. "When I saw the lighthouse I thought, 'oh my gosh, would I ever love to have that,'" says Robertson, who was living in Thunder Bay at the time with her third husband and was considering retirement, her children having all set off on lives of their own. "I never had a romantic interest in lighthouses. But this one was just like Hansel and Gretel."

The pilot indicated that the houses were abandoned, and suggested she speak with the Canadian Coast Guard, who still maintained the lighthouse. "At first [the Coast Guard] said I could never live out there alone," she says. "They said, 'What's an old woman like you going to do out at a lighthouse?' But I've been living in the bush all my life. What's so dangerous about an island with a nice house on it?"

The Coast Guard's Ron Walker still remembers Robertson's request. "I thought she was crazy," he says. "At the time we were getting stations ready for survival quarters for our own staff. A lot of the stations were going solar

Thunder Bay native Maureen Robertson spent parts of fourteen years at Trowbridge Island, living in the old lighthouse keepers' residence on property still maintained by the Canadian Coast Guard.

and the diesels [generators] were shut off. She would have nothing out there … no power, no running water. But she was pretty determined." Walker says it was always "easy" for the Coast Guard to lease its facilities to prospective cottagers on Georgian Bay and Lake Huron, but the isolation of most of its Lake Superior lights made them hesitant to strike up similar arrangements here. "We were never responsible for [the safety of lighthouse lessees]," says Walker. "But you don't want to put them in difficult situations."

In 1994, after months of "hemming and hawing," Robertson says the government granted her three months at Porphyry. "I hired a boat out of Silver Islet and went out there by myself for the summer," she says. "I painted and cleaned everything up … the place looked just smashing. And when the Coast Guard came out to check up on me, I guess I convinced them that I could survive out there."

Robertson created a whimsical outdoor "park" at Porphyry, complete with pastel-pink- and robin-egg-blue-painted cars that were left abandoned on the island from lightkeepers in the 1950s. The island sports a sheltered harbour and dock for landing, which made Robertson's task of getting to and from the island relatively easy. But it also attracted a few less desirable human visitors, and made her feel vulnerable. This coupled with the fact that Porphyry is large enough to support a healthy population of black bears encouraged Robertson to jump at the opportunity to move when the lighthouse at rockbound, predator-free Trowbridge Island became available. "I really loved the woods at Porphyry," she says, "and the house had a wood-burning furnace in the basement so I cut my own firewood. It was a lot warmer there [than at Trowbridge, which doesn't have a working furnace]. But there's less to worry about here."

All summer long, Robertson lives like a desert island castaway. Except for a twelve-foot canoe that she rarely uses, she has no means of venturing off the island. She hardly ever gets visitors; according to her logbook, the odd kayaker or pleasure boater spots the lighthouse and stops in for a look around about once every two weeks. She collects rainwater for laundry and hauls drinking water from Lake Superior. Until her last summer at Trowbridge, when she finally yielded to her children's requests to bring a cellphone, she had no means of contact with the outside world. Her husband has visited her summer retreat only a few times.

Robertson rolls her eyes when she tells me about her three marriages; none of her husbands have shared her sense of adventure and love of the outdoors. Her arrangement with her current spouse is decidedly casual: She spends her summers alone on Trowbridge, and has relented to spent three winters with him in Mesa, Arizona. What she's really dreaming of, however, is a solo trip to China. When I ask her how old she feels, she pauses thoughtfully and replies, "Oh, about forty. But I don't think about age. I just want to be … alive. I'm inquisitive and I love life, and I think that's what keeps me young."

She also craves solitude. If you ask her about it, Robertson will downplay the isolation of life on Trowbridge Island. By all definitions — offshore in the cold, unpredictable waters of Lake Superior, fully exposed to the weather and far from the nearest road — the island is cut off from the rest of the world. A late-season storm pinned her down at Porphyry Island in one of her first years there, forcing her to subsist for a week on a few cans of tuna before her worried husband chartered a helicopter to whisk her back to safety. She admits that there are times she feels utterly alone, but those moments quickly pass. "I will admit every once in a while I think, 'What am I doing out here?'" she says. "But that doesn't last long. I tell myself to suck it up, and it passes. My God, I'm not in the Amazon, you know? It's just Lake Superior."

After lunch, Robertson shows me her "art gallery," the airy building that once served as a workshop for lighthouse keepers and currently stores a vast array of batteries, old hand tools, the remains of a foghorn, and a still-functioning marine radio. Amidst the industrial paraphernalia, Robertson has created a small sitting area where she likes to thumb through old magazines "on days when I don't have anything better to do." The walls of the back room of the workshop are covered with newspaper clippings heralding the exploits of various friends.

One summer, she ventured into the building's dungeon-like cellar and discovered a handwritten note amidst a pile of rusting pipes. It was written by Debbie Kerr, whose parents tended the light in the early 1960s. "The letter was so cute," says Robertson. "I called all of the Kerrs in the [Thunder Bay] phone book and eventually found someone whose sister [Joyce] was Debbie's mother." Robertson has since become friends with Joyce Kerr. "I invited her to come visit me but she said, 'never again … I never want to see a lighthouse for the rest of my life,'" laughs Robertson.

Kerr told Robertson about other secrets of Trowbridge Island, including the chicken coop she shows me after we leave the art gallery and follow a network of trails crisscrossing the rocky spine of the island. Although Trowbridge measures barely three football fields long by about one football field wide, it takes us over an hour to explore paths that tunnel through a dense forest of lichen-draped spruce. Since she finished remodelling the lightkeepers' houses, Robertson has turned her attention to rediscovering the well-worn lightkeeper trails and cutting new ones. Prior to the construction of a concrete pier, the original builders of the lighthouse, residence building, and workshop faced the daunting task of hauling lumber and thousands of tons of cement across the island from a rough landing on the rocky east side. The hardships of the past seem fleeting as Robertson and I stop at places with signposts that read "Garnet Gulch," "Amber Cove," and "Jade Valley" — secret hideaways where she enjoys her morning coffee or kindles evening campfires.

After supper, Robertson gives me the key to the lighthouse and I climb a series of wooden steps to the eight-sided tower atop the crest of the island. It's hot inside the glass dome, the space cramped by the original Fresnel lens, a multi-mirrored optic that resembles an insect's eye and is among the last

The original Fresnel lens, one of the few remaining in Great Lakes lighthouses, fills the lantern room atop the Trowbridge Island lighthouse. A smaller solar-powered light now does the job, its flash visible for approximately thirty kilometres across the water.

of its kind in the Great Lakes. The monstrous Fresnel has been replaced by a cookie jar–sized lamp that's powered by a small solar panel mounted just outside the turret — an effective visual demonstration of the changes in lighthouse technology.

Descending the stairs and following the walkway back to the lightkeepers' duplex, it suddenly strikes me that I'm witnessing the end of an era. When Robertson heard about the Heritage Lighthouses Protection Act and the government's plans to auction off lighthouses to non-profit organizations, she decided that 2010 would be her last year on the island. She says she can't be bothered to draft a petition, collect signatures, and jump through hoops to be Trowbridge's official caretaker. The property needs significant structural work: new subfloors, siding, windows, and a new outhouse, or better yet, a modern septic system. She took Parks Canada's call for petitions as a sign to move on, to spend more time with her grandchildren, travel, or maybe even to find a new "project."

It stuns me to think that in a few short weeks, Robertson will leave her beloved "Gypsy Moth Island" for good. Except for a few keepsakes (including her Ronald Reagan photo), she says, "everything is staying here when I leave." I ask her how she envisions her departure day. She hesitates, and then describes how the helicopter will fly overhead and circle the island before landing. But when it takes off, it will head directly to Thunder Bay. "There's no looking back," she says. "I think I might cry."

I retire to the workshop building where I spread my sleeping bag on the spare bed and try to sleep. But it's impossible to sleep after a day like this. My mind is racing, replaying the scenes, trying to remember the details and saddened by the fact that I'll never be in this magical place again. I hear the dull, droning sound of a freighter that's bound for the Lakehead. From the window, I watch the lights of the ship about a kilometre offshore beneath a waxing late-July moon, its crew no doubt oblivious to the wondrous island they're passing. When the workshop's deep-set fumes of fuel oil force me to move outdoors, I lay down on warm lakeside rocks and let the sound of the waves lull me to sleep.

Trowbridge Island is the kind of place where you're afraid to look at a clock because time goes by so fast. It feels like breakfast is barely over when it's time for lunch. You go for a swim in Lake Superior's bracingly cold water, sit down for afternoon tea, and the next thing you know it's eight o'clock in the evening. You lose track of time because life on this island is so surreal. All too soon, the sun sinks beneath the Sleeping Giant and Trowbridge's lighthouse flashes once every five seconds, its light arcing like a metronome across the dark water; too soon, it's time to leave.

Robertson says every day she spent on Trowbridge went by too fast. All along, she knew her tenure was temporary. "I've always been aware that the Coast Guard could take this from me at any time," she says. "And rightly so. It's their property and they might need it someday." But that didn't allay the sting of her last day.

A month later, I phone Robertson to ask about leaving the island. "It was a little heartbreaking, but I sort of expected that," she says. "The pilot who came to get me was a young guy and he was so cute. He asked if I would like to circle back and see the island one last time. I said, 'Do you really want to make me cry?' I told him to get me out of there fast. I cried when I got home." She says it would be "wonderful" if someone acquires the Trowbridge light-keepers' residence and preserves it under the new heritage legislation. But she cuts me off when I suggest the possibility of a revisiting the island. "I could never go out there again," she says. "It would hurt too much. That place was like a child to me.

"But I've just got to have another project," she continues, her voice rising in excitement. "I have to be out in the woods. I've always yearned for a little cabin in the woods, away from everyone. I'm not afraid … I know I will find it."

CHAPTER 2

The Iceman

Sea-kayaking on the Great Lakes got its start thirty years ago in an unlikely place. Stan Chladek, a Ph.D. chemist and world-class whitewater slalom paddler in his native Czechoslovakia, slipped out of war-torn Eastern Europe just ahead of Soviet tanks of the Iron Curtain and immigrated to the Detroit area in the late 1960s. Frustrated by the Midwest's lack of whitewater paddling, he learned of the popularity of sea-kayaking in the Pacific Northwest and in the British Isles and saw the potential in the vast inland seas in the heart of North America.

Being a dyed-in-the-wool whitewater canoeist, I imagine there was some reluctance when he picked up a double-bladed paddle and launched a sea kayak for the first time. But the sport quickly took root in the Great Lakes, and Chladek was soon selling dozens of boats at his Detroit paddling shop. He was quick a convert and began to discover the wealth of sea-kayaking destinations within an easy drive of his home in southern Michigan. Lake Superior became his favourite place to paddle for its unruly personality, spectacular scenery, remote coastline, and rich First Nations heritage. Always a daredevil, Chladek organized late-season kayak surfing trips to take advantage of the "gales of November" and April "ice-breaker" expeditions to celebrate the arrival of a new season of paddling.

His annual autumn rendezvous on Lake Superior's Agawa Bay, about 140 kilometres north of Sault Ste. Marie, became the stuff of legends. Starting in 1984, a troupe of sea kayakers road-tripped north to endure freak snowstorms, towering waves, and ice-cold water. The harsh elements were tempered with camaraderie in a woodstove-heated canvas tent. The Gales of November Rendezvous climaxed in the 1990s, when fifty-odd paddlers from around the world converged on Agawa Bay. Since then the event has declined — perhaps because of its aging participants. But through all the years, Stan Chladek has yet to miss his annual late-season weekend of sea-kayaking on Lake Superior.

I attended my first Gales of November in 2003, and occasionally participated in the years that followed. In 2009, Chladek surprised me with a phone call and *asked me to help him coordinate a special twenty-fifth anniversary Gales. I recruited a handful of fresh-faced friends and Chladek invited some of the founding participants who had long since retired their sea kayaks and taken up other pursuits. Out of the event came an unspoken pact: The show must go on.*

Chladek is an iron man — hardnosed, outspoken, and, even in his seventies, a well-travelled expedition sea kayaker. He continues to make annual pilgrimages to paddle Alaska's Aleutian Islands, where he's seeking the archeological remains of the original Inuit sea kayakers. But beneath his tough and macho shell, he's a kind, softhearted man who thinks there's nothing better than a day spent sea-kayaking on Lake Superior. With each passing year, I can tell he more greatly cherishes the experience.

On a blustery November night, Stan Chladek is holding court in a crowded, woodsmoke-stained canvas tent, his weathered face and shock of thick grey hair illuminated by the gaudy LCD glow of a laptop computer screen. As unlikely as the scene seems, Chladek, a solidly built, seventy-two-year-old Czech-American, is doing what he does best — recounting tall tales of near misses and high drama from a lifetime of paddling the world's oceans and rivers. In classic Chladek fashion, stories include the statements, "I should've died," "I knew I was going to die," and "I don't know how I didn't die," and are laced with his typical outspoken candor. It seems like his references to death come each time he gulps from one of the many bottles of Captain Morgan's spiced rum that are circulating the tent.

Tonight, Lake Superior is his keynote topic. About twenty-five of us have gathered at the otherwise dark and deserted Lake Superior Provincial Park campground at Agawa Bay, 140 kilometres north of Sault Ste. Marie, for the Gales of November Rendezvous. Chladek organized the first such

Stan Chladek, the father of sea-kayaking on the Great Lakes, revels in cold November water at a gathering in the early 1990s.
Photo courtesy of Stan Chladek.

invitation-only gathering of expert sea kayakers through his Detroit paddling shop twenty-five years ago — about the same time a couple of the tent's youngest faces were born. We chuckle at grainy photos of some of the first sea kayakers on the Great Lakes wearing tacky DayGlo wetsuits and brandishing old-school wooden paddles. In the next breath, we stare slack-jawed at images of the same paddlers surfing giant waves, daringly darting in and out of rocky channels, and touring along the wintry coast in blinding snowstorms. A few of these paddlers are in the audience tonight, their eyes widening and mouths smiling as the father of sea-kayaking on the Great Lakes takes us on a visual tour of the riotous early days.

Upon immigrating to the United States in the late 1960s, Chladek opened Great River Outfitters in a suburb of Detroit a decade later and introduced the sport of sea-kayaking to the Great Lakes. His was the first North American paddle shop to import sleek and slender, rough-water-inspired, British-built sea kayak designs, and to offer paddle-sports training through the notoriously stringent British Canoe Union. At the time, sea-kayaking in North America was a decidedly placid pursuit with roots in the calm, sheltered waters of the Pacific Northwest. But the thrill-seeking Chladek wasn't interested in flatwater. He bought into the British paddlers' tradition of big-wave surfing, playing in treacherous "rock gardens," and embarking on multi-day adventures along exposed coastlines. He converted a few friends, sold boats, and offered courses. Slowly, a new generation of paddlers was born.

The Gales of November Rendezvous, first hosted in 1984 on a gravel beach just south of Lake Superior Provincial Park, was a perfect venue to celebrate this new school of sea-kayaking in the frigidly cold and often rough waters of late fall. In the Gales' heyday in the late 1980s, upwards of fifty paddlers would join Chladek on the first weekend in November on Lake Superior. The coastline is empty at this time of year — the tourist season ending with the last of the fall colours in early October.

For several years, the event drew the likes of well-known Welsh expedition paddler and sea kayak designer Nigel Dennis, sea kayak design pioneer Frank Goodman, and members of California's Tsunami Rangers troupe of surf-kayak fiends. Its reputation as a big-water, testosterone-laced surfer-fest grew in the 1990s before it gradually fell off the paddling radar. But all along, in between sea-kayak expeditions to Easter Island, Antarctica, and the British Isles, Chladek has been a fixture at the Gales.

He planned bigger things for the twenty-fifth anniversary. An email invitation was addressed to a long list of paddlers in late summer; and veteran Sault Ste. Marie, Ontario-based sea kayaker Bruce Lash dug out his old "moose hunting" tent, a mainstay at early Gales, bought a new woodstove, and arrived early to set it up. Lash was one of the "original ten" — a group of ten paddlers who participated in the first ten rendezvous, starting in 1984. "I just like hanging out in a big, warm, canvas prospector tent with a hearty woodstove blazing away, reading a good story and sipping hot chocolate, hiking or paddling only when the weather allows," Lash wrote in a group email. "A few familiar faces would add to the ambiance. In this same tent twenty-three years earlier, we had at least seventeen people gathered around the woodstove after dark. But for the most part, I just like the sheer opposites that a canvas tent can create this time of year. Inside, warm, cozy and dry; outside, windy, cold and hostile."

About twenty-five paddlers showed up from across the American Midwest and Ontario, including a few originals from the first rendezvous. With a forecast of unsettled weather, an overheated canvas wall tent, laptop computer, and healthy supply of Captain Morgan's, the silver anniversary Gales of November Rendezvous was set to begin.

A broken sea kayak greets intrepid paddlers at a Gales of November Rendezvous in the late 1980s. The kayak once belonged to Detroit-based paddler Ron Monkman, and was dashed on the rocks by four-metre waves in a harrowing close call at Sinclair Cove in Lake Superior Provincial Park.

Photo courtesy of Stan Chladek.

. . .

A day at the Gales of November Rendezvous begins as follows: You awake in the cold confines of your tent or the bed of your pickup truck, reluctantly leave your toasty sleeping bag, don copious layers, and walk over to the moose tent for breakfast. The crackling woodstove soon takes the chill out of the air, and before long, Stan Chladek has arrived to announce the day's plans. The tent always falls silent when Chladek speaks. "I think we will go to the pictographs," he says in his inimitable Czech accent. "That is always a nice paddle. Yes, I think that is where we will go."

With that, we scarf down the last of our breakfasts, leave a note on the picnic table for latecomers, and carpool a few minutes north on the Trans-Canada to picture-postcard, granite-rimmed Sinclair Cove, where we will paddle to the Ojibwa pictographs two kilometres south at Agawa Rock and play in the reflection waves along the rugged shores of the neighbouring islands. As I struggle into my cold drysuit in the parking lot before we launch, I'm taken aback by the haunting opening bars of Gordon Lightfoot's "The Wreck of the Edmund Fitzgerald," coming from the cassette deck of Traverse City, Michigan, paddler Dave Dickerson's beat-up sedan. For a moment, there's nothing but the sound of Lightfoot's ballad in the parking lot. But reverie is interrupted by hoots of laughter. Chladek has arrived and emerges from his Suburu wearing a grotesque Halloween mask, a long-standing Gales tradition.

Despite his age, Chladek is still a powerful sea kayaker, and he digs resolutely into a stiff twenty-knot headwind when we get on the water. He chatters non-stop, telling me about his plans to embark next summer on yet another sea-kayak expedition to the Aleutian Islands in the Alaskan Arctic, his anticipation of spending the winter downhill-skiing in his new home in Colorado, and his most recent trip to paddle the Mediterranean. But his words become sparse when we reach the ancient pictographs on the sheer forty-metre face of Agawa Rock. "That's what keeps me coming back to this lake," he whispers, gesturing toward the faded, blood red rendition of Mishepeshu, the great horned lynx and restless Ojibwa water-god.

We round the rugged Agawa Islands and head north, beyond Sinclair Cove and to the site of the Gales' biggest mishap. The 1989 rendezvous was memorably rough, with gale-force winds and three-metre swells rolling into the typically sheltered cove. Two-storey waves battered the outer islands.

Only a handful of paddlers took to the water. "I remember thinking, 'this is crazy,'" Lash tells me, reflecting on the day. "I left my boat on the roof of the car and went hiking instead. I didn't want to be anywhere near the water that day. I didn't want to be called in to testify at a coroner's inquest."

Today, as we visit the site of his near demise, Detroit paddler Ron Monkman remembers the four-metre wave that surfed him into a rocky headland, which split his boat in two and left him struggling to survive in the foaming ice-cold water. "Huge waves were beating me into the rock," he says. "I had almost given up hope and was prepared to die." Somehow, Chladek managed to extricate Monkman from the fray and hauled him on the back deck of his kayak toward the mainland shore. Michigan paddler Dave Ide, who was then one of the highest-ranking sea-kayaking coaches in North America, crash-landed and was able to pull the battered swimmer onto the rocks with a rope. It's hard to believe that somewhere beneath us lay the tail of the busted boat. After a bruised and hypothermic Monkman was windlassed to safety, Chladek and company towed the bow of his kayak into the sheltered cove "like a funeral procession."

Our tour is less dramatic. The once-promising wind dies off and in twos and threes we paddle back to the parking lot, our surf helmets still strapped to the decks of our kayaks, and caravan back to the campground. It seems almost fitting that Chladek bemoans the loss of old-time rough-water sea-kayaking in the moose tent that night. "Who is going to organize this next year?" he laments over an empty rum bottle, after almost everyone has gone off to bed. "I am afraid there are no *real* paddlers anymore. I am still here, but it won't be long before I make the trip to the geriatric hospital."

On Saturday morning, a steady northwest swell lashes the coast and a few of us wake up early to prove Chladek wrong. I shuttle north to Katherine Cove with my wife Kim, sea-kayak guides and stalwart friends Ray Boucher, Dave Wells, Ginny Marshall, Vince Paquot, and Michigan-based photographer Greg Maino, another young, solid paddler and great guy. Predictable, glassy sets roll into a sand beach, offering exceptional surf. The biggest waves are head-high or better — the perfect size for surfing a sea kayak.

Surfing in long boats like these isn't easy. My sixteen-foot "touring" kayak is a behemoth compared to shorter, surfboard-inspired surf kayaks or bathtub-sized whitewater kayaks, and therefore far less manoeuvrable and harder to control. The biggest challenge in surfing "a long boat" is dealing with its tendency to broach — for its bow to dig in and fling the kayak sideways. But for me the challenge is the greatest appeal. There's nothing faster than a sea kayak riding down the face of a big wave; the sensation of surfing a long boat is akin to flying. We play hard all morning, catching some long rides, broaching, rolling, and getting tossed over the handlebars in dramatic "enders" when caught in the wrong place at the wrong time. When Chladek arrives in time for a late lunch after a paddle down the coast of his own, he seems pleased with our exploits.

There's a powerful sense of camaraderie in the moose tent that night as Chladek shows slides on his laptop and tells stories. The setting is surreal, with the computer screen casting a strange, pale glow on the flapping tent walls. But despite the incongruity of the scene, or maybe because of it, I feel like I'm a part of a tradition that's been shaped by the ice-cold water and buffeting fall winds of Lake Superior, and is still going strong.

By the end of the night, there's an energy pulsing through the tent that suggests the twenty-fifth Gales of November Rendezvous won't be the last. Slowly, the crowd thins and I ask Chladek if he ever imagined himself doing a slide show in a mouldy old tent on the coast of Lake Superior. "That's interesting," he says, pausing to reflect. "I guess when I started the Gales I never thought it would last this long." I shove another piece of wood into the cherry-red stove, blasting more heat into the tent. "You know, this has been a good Gales," Chladek says. "Maybe we will do it next year. Maybe I will be here."

The author surfs a sixteen-foot sea kayak in Lake Superior surf in early September. The lake tends to be roughest in autumn and three- to five-metre swells are not uncommon.
Photograph by Kim Mihell.

CHAPTER 3

Between a Rock and a Hard Place

Lake Superior has a way of making human endeavours seem trivial and nowhere else does that feeling ring truer than at Michipicoten, an arrowhead-shaped bay on the lake's eastern shore. The Michipicoten River pours into the bay in a seething mass of swirling eddies, shifting sandbars, and, if Lake Superior is rough, walls of towering breakers. To the south and north, the sheer cliffs that gave the place its Ojibwa name stretch to the horizon. The only things breaking the emptiness is the Michipicoten Lighthouse on Perkwakwia Point and Michipicoten Island, sixty-five kilometres distant, whose contours it seems are only visible in the hours leading up to a rainstorm.

It's hard to imagine that Michipicoten was once an industrial hub. Rival Hudson's Bay Company and North West Company posts sprung up in the fur trade, vying for control over the main route to James Bay via the Michipicoten, Missinaibi, and Moose rivers. Later, its sheltered harbour served as a deepwater port for the lake freighters that hauled iron ore from the mines in Wawa to the steel mill in Sault Ste. Marie. At the turn of the century, Michipicoten Harbour was home to over five hundred people.

All vestiges of the fur-trading posts and most of the harbour infrastructure had disappeared when a U.S. firm purchased the old ore docks in 1999. Detroit-based Carlos Companies planned to blast shoreline rocks into "trap rock," a high-grade road-building aggregate, to be shipped stateside for construction projects. With the majority of townspeople in support of the hundred-odd jobs Superior Aggregates initially promised, environmentalists were squarely in the crosshairs when they exposed a number of sizeable cracks in the developer's plans. Moments of tension came in waves, culminating in May 2009 when an open house as part of an Ontario Municipal Board hearing to render a final decision on the project ended in threats and catcalls. Ultimately, the quasi-judicial board gave Superior Aggregates the go-ahead. By this time, the proponent had reeled in its initial job projections to only twelve employees.

The global economic recession has since stalled the quarry, easing the storm and maintaining peace at Michipicoten. I've been on close terms with the issue since the quarry plans were first revealed in 2002, as a seasonal employee in the tourism industry and as a resident of Wawa and Michipicoten Bay. At the height of the debate in 2008 I wrote about it for the Globe and Mail; *being so close to the debate made my reportage both easy in terms of finding sources and research material and difficult in maintaining objectivity. In this story I have excerpted from and updated my previous work in the* Globe *and* Cottage Life *magazine.*

The droning diesel engine of the *John A.* punctures the spring fog of Lake Superior. The sound is reassuring, though I'm still questioning my sanity. What was I thinking when I decided to solo a canoe across the big lake's open water? Now I'm rolling in the swell and taking my chances with a wall of fog that threatens to swallow my return route.

On a day like this, it would be easy to mistake Michipicoten Bay cottager Ken Mills's vessel for the ghost of the *Edmund Fitzgerald*. But as the

Over the years, Michipicoten Harbour cottager and Wawa local Ken Mills has reclaimed an old commercial fishery with structures salvaged from as far as Sault Ste. Marie. His cherished lifeboat, the John A., *is moored to the dock. It travelled through the Northwest Passage aboard a Canadian icebreaker in 1969.*

fifty-four-passenger, double-ended steel lifeboat takes shape in the mist, I recognize Mills's wiry, eighty-two-year-old frame at the helm, tufts of salt-and-pepper hair curling out from under the sides of his cap. I volunteered to paddle out from a friend's place on the Michipicoten River and meet Mills in the middle of the bay to pick up a dozen fillets of smoked trout I had watched him prepare at his water-access cottage the day before. When our two vessels meet, he passes a cardboard box of fish over the *John A.*'s rail, we chat for a minute, then say goodbye. The romantic appeal of an old captain firing up the diesel and turning his lifeboat back toward the fog-cloaked harbour is lost on me; I'm too preoccupied with digging deep and sprinting for the safety of shore.

Yesterday, I spent the better part of a morning with the vigorous seafarer at his cottage, where Mills revealed to me his "secret blend" marinade for smoked trout before stuffing a fridge-sized smoker full of fresh-caught fillets. Then we shared a pot of tea steeped on a wood-burning stove while he told me stories of his life on Lake Superior. Mills grew up barely a kilometre away in Michipicoten Harbour, near the northern Ontario town of Wawa. He remembers a time, seventy-some years ago, when dozens of loggers, trappers, miners, and railway workers lived with their families in the harbour, and Great Lakes freighters docked at its now-sagging pier to take on loads of iron ore, pulpwood, and lumber. Mills acquired the lease on his province-owned land in the early 1950s from a local fisherman and became one of the area's first cottagers. Over the years, he has barged in scavenged materials from condemned buildings and wharves as far away as Sault Ste. Marie, creating a haphazard series of docks, sheds, and cabins that give his "camp" the feel of a maritime outport.

Mills spends most of his time alone at the cottage. His wife, Shirley, comes out from their home in Wawa on the weekends, and children and grandchildren visit in the summer. "There's no end to the work," he says, referring to his constant need to jury-rig repairs to heaving docks and rotting sheds, and the annual chore of hauling, splitting, and stacking firewood by hand. "But I like it. It's a bit of a bone of contention with my family but I like being here alone and working. Shirley and I argue about how much time I spend at camp, but I try to be here most of the summer and come out at least once every two weeks over the ice in the winter.

"When I'm too old to walk in the water to fix the docks or climb up on the roof to patch the shingles," he adds, "I don't know what I will do."

Mills's stubborn independence is typical of Michipicoten Bay residents, who are, by and large, rugged individualists perched on the edge of the wilderness with a common respect and love for the lake. The place has a utopian feel seldom associated with Lake Superior. Old-timers like Mills have watched this idyll descend on the bay as the industrial hub of Michipicoten Harbour decayed and the last iron ore–laden freighter chugged out of the port, leaving a paradise of sand and clear water in its wake. But like the occasional storms that still claim lives, sink vessels, and damage property, a rumbling of change threatens the community. Wawa locals, stricken with a long-depressed economy, support an aggregate quarry that could redevelop the harbour. The Lake Superior ecosystem as a whole and the glacial microclimate isolated on this part of the lake's shore are showing signs of change. Time will tell how the bay and the people — both hardy and resilient — will respond.

Michipicoten Bay barely registers as a horseshoe-shaped indentation on the eastern shore of the largest freshwater lake in the world. Lake Superior has an area of 82,100 square kilometres and Michipicoten takes up about two thousand of them. Its focal point is the west-flowing Michipicoten River, which bisects sand and pebble beaches and jagged, teal-coloured rock headlands until it melds with the watery horizon. Heading north of the river mouth, the majority of the bay's thirty-odd cottages and year-round homes line Long Beach. Beyond another rock headland is Sandy Beach, a less densely developed stretch of fine sand and wispy dune grass. Perkwakwia Point, with its metal-framed lighthouse and classic, red-roofed lightkeepers' bungalows dwarfed by cliffs of three-billion-year-old volcanic greenstone bedrock, protrudes from the northwest corner of the bay, marking the entrance to Michipicoten Harbour. Ken Mills's place, located just north of the lighthouse, is one of the few cottages on this part of the bay.

On the south side of the river, the three-kilometre sweep of Driftwood Beach is protected entirely by Michipicoten Post Provincial Park; and past that, towering cliffs of Crown land extend six kilometres to the boundary of Lake Superior Provincial Park. The view is spectacular regardless of where you stand on the bay: rockbound coastline reminiscent of the Maritimes meets massive sand beaches, and the crystalline blue waters of Lake Superior stretch to a prairie-like horizon. It's no surprise then that Group of Seven painter A.Y.

The sun sets over Michipicoten Harbour, where a Michigan-based aggregate company proposed to blast shoreline rock into road-building materials. In the distance lies 180 kilometres of wilderness coastline protected by provincial conservation reserves and Pukaskwa National Park.

Jackson once owned a log cabin on Sandy Beach and famed Toronto-based pianist and composer Glenn Gould also made annual retreats to Michipicoten for inspiration.

When Michipicoten cottager Mary Jo Cullen discovered the area with her partner, Torfinn Hansen, in the mid-1980s, her first experience belied Superior's reputation for nastiness. The pair had just descended the wild whitewater rapids of the Dog River by canoe, flushing into the lake thirty kilometres west of Michipicoten. They expected the icy fog and oceanic waves that Lake Superior is famous for, but on that day it was peaceful and fog-free, and the water was easily warm enough for swimming. She fell in love. "It was as if this place was somehow forgotten. I'd been to the beaches of the Mediterranean in the sixties, where people were packed in body-to-body. But here we have all this sand to ourselves. There are no footprints, just signs of the waves. It's like stepping back in time."

The couple returned annually, eventually purchasing a tiny fourteen-by-eighteen-foot cabin atop a promontory south of Long Beach. It was built in 1967 by Mickey Clement, a Wawa craftsman who is said to have put up more than three hundred such log structures in northeastern Ontario with the logs standing vertically, a rough yet functional design he pioneered to make best use of the stunted, twiggy conifers of the boreal forest. That same northern forest — wind-wizened black spruce and a sea of waist-high Labrador tea — hides the cabin from the water.

The cottages and year-round homes on the bay represent the only human habitation along eastern Lake Superior. Northwest of Wawa, the Trans-Canada Highway cuts far inland, creating a two-hundred-kilometre stretch of wilderness from Michipicoten to the town of Marathon. To the south, Lake Superior Provincial Park protects another 120 kilometres of coastline.

Best guess, based on the work of archaeologists who have unearthed layers of Aboriginal and European artifacts ranging from arrowheads to flintlock guns, is that Ojibwa people lived seasonally on the dunes of Driftwood Beach at the river mouth for some three thousand years. The Ojibwa word *Michipicoten* translates to "big bluffs," and likely refers to the cliffs on the south side of the bay. It is one of the oldest Ontario place names adopted by Europeans, first appearing on Samuel de Champlain's map of 1632. For early explorers and then fur traders, Michipicoten was a critical link between the Great Lakes and the Arctic Ocean, via a seven-hundred-kilometre-long canoe route to James Bay. In 1725, French traders established a post a kilometre upstream on the Michipicoten River. It changed hands through various business mergers until the Hudson's Bay Company finally boarded it up in 1904. Just like the old community at Michipicoten Harbour, all that's left of the old fur-trading post is a grassy field.

Torfinn Hansen is still overcome with youthful enthusiasm every time he loads up his station wagon with power tools, two golden retrievers, and his cherished torpedo-shaped sea kayak and drives twelve hours north from his home in Toronto to the Michipicoten Bay property he purchased in 1997. "It's a primitive urge for me," he says, "to come up here and be in contact with the big water. I grew up with the sounds of the ocean; the sounds of Lake Superior are very much the same."

Hansen is built like a sparkplug — strong and compact — and barely showing his sixty-nine years. Born in the Faroe Islands, a North Atlantic archipelago halfway between Scotland and Iceland, he's the product of generations of precision woodworkers and machinists, so it's no surprise that he's a retired high school shop teacher. At the cottage, he spends most of his time in his own workshop, a converted Viceroy-style building with exposed roof beams and a wall of windows, where he tinkers with construction projects the way only a perfectionist can.

Hansen's dream is to move north full-time. Cullen, his "soul mate," bought into the plan after she completed two summer-long solo circumnavigations of Lake Superior's two-thousand-kilometre coastline by sea kayak. "When I finished my second trip around the lake there was no doubt in my mind we'd be moving up here," she says. The pair then spent a winter at Michipicoten about ten years ago, hauling lake water by hand up an icy rock cliff and endlessly stoking a cooktop-woodstove. "We absolutely loved it," says Cullen. "We had this little cabin and terrific plans for the future." The following summer Hansen cut, peeled, and stacked spruce logs to build an addition that would make the one-room cottage more comfortable for year-round use.

But then, in 2002, Hansen and Cullen caught wind of a U.S. company's plans to build a quarry near the former ore docks in Michipicoten Harbour. "Any hesitation I have about moving north comes from the quarry," admits Cullen. She has since become involved in other environmental battles as a member of southern Ontario-based aggregate watchdog Gravel Watch and Freshwater Future, a Great Lakes water-quality organization based in Michigan. Meanwhile, Hansen's pile of carefully peeled spruce logs teeters in the driveway, each year becoming more weather-worn.

With layoffs and shutdowns at area lumber mills like the Weyerhaeuser press-board plant, which left over 130 people out of work late in 2007, pickings have been slim for Wawa for over a decade. So in 2002, when Superior Aggregates Company (SAC), a subsidiary of the Michigan-based highway-building giant Carlo Companies, proposed to redevelop the harbour across from Ken Mills's camp as an aggregate quarry and processing facility, most of the community was very much in favour. Longtime residents of Wawa understand firsthand the economic boon of mining — the town sprung up in the wake of an 1898 gold rush, was supported by iron-ore mines for nearly a century, and has experienced the booms and busts of mineral discoveries all along.

In this case, SAC proposed clearing vegetation on a 386-hectare site in the harbour to within sixty metres of the Lake Superior shoreline in order to blast away the underlying three-billion-year-old rock into high-grade gravel. The land was formerly owned by Algoma Steel, which shipped Wawa iron ore to its mill in Sault Ste. Marie by freighter on Lake Superior. In 1999, a year after the Algoma Ore Division ceased operations in Wawa, SAC purchased the property for US$725,000. It contains trap rock, which is far more valuable to road builders than the typical crushed limestone aggregates from quarries on, say, the Niagara Escarpment because of its durability. Furthermore, the company could cut costs significantly by shipping the aggregate from an existing 450-metre-long wharf.

According to consultant reports, SAC would remove up to 23,000 tonnes of material a week and provide permanent seasonal jobs to about a dozen people during the first phase of operation, which would last five to ten years. Profits generated during the initial phase would be used to upgrade the wharf and research the feasibility of expanding operations. In 2004, the company applied to the Ontario Ministry of Natural Resources (MNR) to develop a quarry, but "it was determined that the groundwater elevation was closer to the surface ... than was previously thought." SAC then reapplied for a permit to quarry beneath the water table.

SAC consultant Harold Chelay of DST Consulting was upbeat in early 2008 when I interviewed him about the project, which he claimed was poised to begin. "The concerns of government agencies have been dealt with and we're responding to objections from the public," said Chelay. "The community needs something energetic and new to start up. I'd say 98 percent of the population supports it."

Among Chelay's 2 percent who objected to the quarry were Hansen and Cullen, who challenged the project independently, and Joel Cooper, a member of the Citizens Concerned for Michipicoten Bay (CCMB), a group of full-time and seasonal residents who have been "caring for the coast" since 2002. Among those supporting the citizens group's position are environmental advocacy organizations such as Gravel Watch Ontario, Environmental Defence Canada, and Freshwater Future.

Cooper's humble year-round home of more than twenty-five years on Sandy Beach is separated from SAC's property by two kilometres of Canadian Shield and the boreal forest immortalized by A.Y. Jackson's famous paintings. All Cooper's group wants, he says, is to ensure that the area's clean water and air continue to provide habitat for fish and wildlife, and remain attractive to residents and tourists alike. The noise of pit quarrying, the risk of water contamination due to dust and leaching, and the visual impact of stripping the land and blasting the rock do not fit the group's vision.

Of most concern is the fact that, under existing legislation, SAC will need to assess the potential environmental effects only on the 10 percent of its land that it has applied for a licence to quarry. Yet if it plans to be in operation over the long haul, Cooper says, it will have to apply to expand its area of operations within five years. "It's a 'foot-in-the-door' strategy where the hope is future approvals won't come with the same degree of scrutiny," he says. "We'd rather examine the long-term, cumulative impacts now, rather than in phases over the next fifty years."

In 2004, Cooper's group presented the Ontario Ministry of the Environment (MOE) with 4,600 letters of support for an inspection under the provincial Environmental Assessment Act. Instead, the province extended the jurisdiction of the Aggregate Resources Act, which is managed by the MNR and until then had encompassed only southern Ontario; the act now includes the development at Michipicoten, but it is fundamentally different from the Environmental Assessment Act.

Joel Cooper stands on greenstone bedrock at Rock Island, at the mouth of the Michipicoten River. Cooper has lived in a small house on Michipicoten Bay since the early 1980s.

To acquire a licence to quarry under the act, an applicant must provide a site plan and documents outlining land use, the type and amount of aggregate to be removed, and rehabilitation plans, as well as technical reports dealing with environmental, cultural, and hydrological considerations. These materials are then assessed by municipal, provincial, and federal agencies. The applicant is also required to notify and consult the public and attempt to mediate any objections before being able to proceed with a development.

"The act is sound, but it presumes that the MNR has exclusive control when other laws such as the Environmental Protection Act should apply as well," says Ric Holt, president of Gravel Watch Ontario. "The rules might make sense in some contexts, but it's not at all clear that they apply on the north shore of Lake Superior."

Cooper says the applicant-driven Aggregate Resources Act "isn't the appropriate piece of legislation" because it facilitates SAC's piecemeal approach to developing its property and is too narrow in its environmental scope. "They're only required to look at impacts within one hundred and twenty metres of the proposed site," he says. "But the impact is going to go well beyond one hundred and twenty metres, especially on Lake Superior."

The situation at Michipicoten Bay bears an uncanny resemblance to a standoff at Digby Neck, Nova Scotia, in 2002, when a New Jersey–based road-building conglomerate proposed a quarry of similar proportions on the shore of the North Atlantic. That bid was snuffed out in 2007 by the provincial Department of Environment and Labour because of "unacceptable risks to the environment and communities."

In Nova Scotia, worry about the proposed quarry's threats to fisheries and a burgeoning tourism industry outweighed the promise of twenty-odd jobs. But in Wawa, concerned citizen calls for a similar comprehensive environmental assessment were ignored. Instead, the project went before the Ontario Municipal Board, a quasi-judicial land-use planning agency that's notoriously developer-friendly, in the spring of 2009. After several months of deliberations, the SAC project received the official go-ahead.

Even at the height of summer, there are no docks and decks along the water's edge at Michipicoten, a hint of the lake's destructive power. But it is in late summer and autumn that Superior best lives up to its wicked reputation, when two-storey combers crash like thunder and surf sweeps Sandy and Long beaches clean. Steve Newmaster, a botanist and professor of biology at the University of Guelph, who has spent decades studying the unique flora of the Lake Superior coast, remains amazed by the ability of seemingly delicate vegetation to survive such a rugged environment. Cold-climate flowers, ferns, and mosses typically found in the Arctic or at alpine elevations, cling tenaciously to exposed bedrock all along Lake Superior's north shore. They are the relics of a glacial microclimate that has persisted along the lakeshore since the last ice age, eight thousand years ago. Hidden among Michipicoten Bay's serrated rock outcroppings, the most prevalent plant is encrusted saxifrage (*Saxifraga aizoon*), diminutive and cactus-like, with waxy leaves and long-stemmed, feathery flowers that bloom in July.

Like the voyageurs two hundred years earlier, Steve and his wife, Joan, first saw Michipicoten by canoe. On the Lake Superior leg of a six-thousand-kilometre cross-Canada canoe trip in 1986, Joan suggested they detour into the bay to spend a night on Sandy Beach visiting an old acquaintance. As they paddled between a rock point and an offshore islet just north of Long Beach, Steve remembers glimpsing a small cottage on the point and feeling that he'd discovered paradise. "It was an introduction to our cottage," he says. "In an entire summer of canoeing, Lake Superior was the highlight by far. We knew Michipicoten was a place to return to."

In 1993, the couple purchased the cottage they had eyed on their canoe trip, a bare-bones place tucked in a copse of cedar and spruce. It lacks running water and indoor plumbing. Water is pumped from the lake to a cistern or, in the common event of mechanical breakdown, is hauled by hand. Steve, Joan, and their two daughters, Annabel and Candice, then four and five, lived for twelve months in their cottage the year they bought it. "I was writing a book at the time, and I couldn't think of a better place to do it," says Steve. "We would snowshoe with the kids to the bus stop at minus forty, and only had an outhouse. We have tough children … they still tell us they loved it." Steve's daughters have been his most dedicated research partners at Michipicoten. Now both University of Guelph undergraduate students, they have been collecting lake water temperatures for science fair projects since grade school.

Annabel and Candice's temperature readings echo the findings of their father's colleagues at the University of Minnesota-Duluth: Lake Superior's water temperature has risen a startling two-and-a-half degrees Celsius in the

Among the most common "arctic disjunct" plants found on the Lake Superior coastline is encrusted saxifrage (Saxifraga aizoon), a hardy, succulent plant typically found at alpine elevations or at arctic latitudes. Lake Superior's perennially cold waters produce a micro-climate that's allowed several disjunctive species of vegetation to persist outside of their typical range since the end of the last ice age.

past twenty-five years. Steve's research suggests that the unique shoreline vegetation is already being affected by the warming climate. He says that in the past twenty years, arctic-alpine plant populations have been reduced by 50 to 70 percent. "We've had the same plants living along the coast for the last six thousand to eight thousand years, but in a very short span they've become harder and harder to find."

Steve worries about the change that will take place within his daughters' lifetime, and how that change will affect their connection to Lake Superior. "The cottage has always been the common ground. Just about every three years we've moved somewhere different because of my career, so to our daughters, Michipicoten is home."

I grew up on Lake Superior, too, at my grandparents' cottage just north of Sault Ste. Marie. I know better than to define the lake with stereotypical clichés of deep, unswimmable cold water, storms, and shipwrecks. But on this June morning, as I paddle back from my rendezvous with Ken Mills, the lake shows its more malignant side. The fog rolls across the water and into the hills like gauze

An October storm lashes Government Dock Beach with combers. Unbelievably, a nearby wharf once survived such onslaughts and was critical in bringing people and supplies to nearby Wawa. Scarcely any ruins remain of the old dock, which was located just north of the Michipicoten River.

and my hands are numb from the ice-cold water. I've forgotten my compass and I'm paddling as hard as I can for shore before it becomes obscured in the mist.

Then, as if on cue, the fog lifts minutes after I touch down on a pea-gravel beach just north of the mouth of the river. The capricious lake is silent, and hot early-summer sunshine pierces the clouds — a sudden about-face in weather, typical of life on Lake Superior.

I still visit Mills whenever I have the chance, to share a pot of tea and talk about our mutual interests in Lake Superior. Two years after SAC received its final approval to begin blasting away the rock in the harbour, the property remains abandoned, its pier rotting into the lake and greenstone cliffs as stoic as ever. No doubt the global economic recession impacted the company's plans for quarrying, but skeptics like Torfinn Hansen have other ideas. While plans for the quarry stagnate, Hansen has never given up in his efforts to prove that the idea won't work. Recently, he came up with a theory supported by southern Ontario-based aggregate experts that the much-touted road-building rock SAC sought to blast, grind, and ship away is actually worthless. SAC could be yet another example of the false hopes and promises imparted by the resource exploitation sector on job-starved northern communities.

Meanwhile, the threats of climate change are more insidious. Research led by physicist Jay Austin at the University of Minnesota-Duluth's Large Lakes Observatory revealed that Lake Superior water temperatures reached an all-time high in 2010. While frail flowers wither in the heat of a warming planet, it's likely that the tough and self-reliant residents of Michipicoten Bay, people who embark on marathon canoe trips, venture alone across the ice in the depth of winter, and take pride in cutting wood and hauling water, will adapt. It's hard to imagine them being defeated by the impending changes to the bay.

"The lake shapes the type of people up here," says Cullen, who cherishes more than ever her time on the bay and still holds out hope of living with Lake Superior year-round. "Other places, ones where the winds are sweet and benevolent, don't challenge you very much … maybe that's one of the reasons why we love it."

CHAPTER 4

Treasured Islands

When it comes to deciding on my favourite sea kayak trip on Lake Superior, it's a coin toss between the 125-kilometre-long island chain between the Sibley Peninsula and the village of Rossport and the remote coastline of Pukaskwa National Park. Both trips are vastly different. The Sibley trip is defined by open-water crossings and cobblestone island campsites, while the Pukaskwa features huge sand beaches and intimidating granite headlands. It seems like the Canadian government shares my indecision: national protected areas encompass both stretches of coastline.

Because of its proximity to Thunder Bay and the popular cruising waters of Isle Royale, the Sibley-to-Rossport coastline sees more human traffic than the remote Pukaskwa coast. Despite seeing the odd cottage and pleasure boat, it's still a seriously wild section of coast. But it also feels imperiled. A cursory glance at a Lakehead realty website reveals a handful of properties for sale in northwestern Lake Superior, giving one the impression that as global warming continues to heat up the lake, this area could someday be the next Georgian Bay. Over the course of several years of travelling this section of coastline, I saw cottages pop up on some of my favourite campsites, witnessed the garbage and mess of increased visitation, and experienced rising tensions between pleasure boaters and paddlers vying for the same safe harbours for overnights.

It was for these reasons that I saw the newly minted Lake Superior National Marine Conservation Area as a boon to the long-term survival of this section of coastline. But like any government initiative attempting to balance the desires of a vast array of stakeholders, it is rife with compromise. Until recently, several large and ecologically significant islands within the reserve were up for sale to potential developers, loggers, or mineral exploration companies. Now, while the federal government surveys the area and hashes out its first management plan, the biggest conservation news is coming from grassroots organizations like the Nature Conservancy of Canada and the Thunder Bay Field Naturalists. I'm pleased to report that the future of the island paradise that is northwestern Lake Superior is as bright as ever.

• • •

When the hot, late-afternoon sun beats down on Paradise Island in July, Lake Superior feels more like the Mediterranean. Warmth emanates from a terra-cotta shore of sandstone cobbles and rises like waves on the lake. Beyond the storm line of driftwood, bonsai trees emerge from deep green ground cover. It's only when I walk inland, sinking knee-deep in lush sphagnum and filling my mouth with blueberries, that I remember I'm still at home in northern Ontario.

I launched my sea kayak at Silver Islet, a tiny community at the tip of the Sibley Peninsula, planning to spend a week paddling the 125 kilometres of northwestern Lake Superior coastline to Rossport, a village located two hundred highway kilometres east of Thunder Bay. I reach Paradise Island on my fourth day. I passed dozens of islands along the way, but none are as nice — or as aptly named — as Paradise. The island rises from Lake Superior in a series of terraces; each fifty-centimetre-high step was formed as the earth slowly rebounded from the massive weight of the ice sheets of the last ice age and millennia of storms tossed and shifted the apple-sized stones into distinct beach levels. Even now, the landscape continues to rise in a process known as "isostatic rebound," lifting at a rate of approximately thirty centimetres per century, meaning that the current waterline will one day be represented by a terrace at a much higher elevation.

Exploring further inland, I discover that the step-like pattern continues beyond the treeline, hidden beneath the greenery of succession, forming the foundation of the entire twenty-eight-hectare island that began its rise from the lake some ten thousand years ago. The vegetation is sparse, stunted, and wind-wizened — typical of the sort found in the subarctic or at alpine eleva-tions due to the perennially chilly Lake Superior water, which creates a similarly cool microclimate. On account of its sweeping sandstone beaches — anomalies on Lake Superior — and unique vegetation, Paradise Island was designated an Area of Natural & Scientific Interest (ANSI) by the Ontario Ministry of Natural Resources in 1988.

After admiring the surprisingly hardy three-toothed cinquefoil (*Sibbaldiopsis tridentata*) — a wispy herb with white flowers normally found sixteen hundred kilometres to the north — I return to my campsite and pitch my tent on cobbles just beyond the lake's grasp. As evening falls, I consider what the future holds for Paradise Island. This portion of northwestern Lake Superior has been declared

*Typically found in the Canadian Arctic, knotted pearlwort (*Sagina nodosa*) is a diminutive, wispy, sedge-like plant that has survived since the last ice age in the cool microclimate surrounding Lake Superior. It's common in the Lake Superior National Marine Conservation Area; however, botanists are concerned that rapidly warming water temperatures may make such "arctic disjunct" species casualties of climate change.*

Canada's first National Marine Conservation Area (NMCA), but last I heard, Paradise Island was for sale, listed in the back pages of a regional magazine with an asking price of half a million dollars, and thus excluded from the marine park's protective embrace.

As much as the NMCA designation is cause for celebration, there is also some reason for concern. After years of lobbying Canada to create the world's largest freshwater protected area by the environmental community, the question remains. Has the federal government has gone far enough? Many important areas within the NMCA boundaries have been omitted from protection, including the untamed island on which I've pitched my tent. As much as these unprotected areas could one day become cottage developments, others could be logged for pulpwood, mined for uranium, or quarried for aggregates. It turns out that even after being awarded NMCA status, the wilderness of northwestern Lake Superior remains vulnerable.

In October 2007, Prime Minister Stephen Harper ended a decade of deliberations and political limbo by announcing the approval of the Lake Superior NMCA. The diamond-shaped reserve sprawls across 10,850 square kilometres of northwestern Lake Superior — an area nearly half the size of Georgian Bay — from the tip of the Sibley Peninsula at the mouth of Thunder Bay, to Bottle Point, east of the town of Terrace Bay. The southern boundary follows the Canada–United States border. Despite its distinction as the world's largest freshwater marine park, the NMCA protects barely 13 percent of Lake Superior's 82,100-square-kilometre surface area.

This is the first such protected area to be established under the Canada National Marine Conservation Area Act, which in 2002 enshrined the importance of protecting "self-regulating marine ecosystems ... for the main-tenance of biological diversity." Parks Canada's Doug Yurick says that under this act, the flora, fauna, and structure of northwestern Lake Superior — including the lakebed, water column, and sixty square kilometres of islands and mainland coast — will be safeguarded indefinitely from the exploration and exploitation of oil and gas, mineral, and aggregate resources, as well the dumping of waste products. Similar to a national park, the Lake Superior NMCA must have a management plan in place within the first five years of its designation, which will then be reviewed every five years in parliament.

Yurick says shipping, pleasure boating, and commercial and recreational fishing — all of which are allowed by the act — will be overseen by existing agencies, such as the Ontario Ministry of Natural Resources (MNR) and Transport Canada. Ultimately, he says the overall objective of a NMCA is to "protect the structure and function of the ecosystem while allowing ecologically sustainable use to continue." However, the act also requires zoning to accommodate the "ecologically sustainable use of marine resources."

The island archipelago and open water of northwestern Lake Superior were identified as a potential federal marine park in 1997 for their unique 250-metre-tall sedimentary cliffs, terraced beaches, and approximately twenty-five species of plant life, such as three-toothed cinquefoil, encrusted saxifrage (*Saxifraga aizoon*), and knotted pearlwort (*Sagina nodosa*), which are typically found in the colder climate of the Canadian Arctic or alpine elevations. According to the MNR's Natural Heritage Information Centre, the area provides habitat for about seventy species of rare or at-risk plant life, including devil's club (*Oplopanax horridus*), a thorny, metre-high, broadleafed plant that's typically found in the Rocky Mountains.

"At first you wonder why many of the plants on these islands aren't in your guidebook," says Parks Canada's Gail Jackson, the Lake Superior NMCA's first project manager. "Then you realize the biting cold water of Lake Superior has perpetuated communities of vegetation typical of the far north."

Species of note also include cliff-nesting peregrine falcons and coaster brook trout, an anadromous fish that spends most of its life in Lake Superior and reproduces each autumn in a select few tributaries with upwelling springs of specific temperatures. According to Rob Swainson, a MNR biologist in the Nipigon District, coaster brook trout habitat has been altered so extensively by logging, mining, and road development that Lake Superior's only self-sustaining population exists in Nipigon Bay, part of the new NMCA. The reserve also protects Gapen's Pool on the Nipigon River, which Swainson says is the most prolific spawning area for coaster brook trout in the entire Lake Superior basin. MNR research suggests that the area contains about a dozen species of fauna with rare or at-risk status, while 290 species of birds have been observed at the Thunder Cape Bird Observatory, located at the western terminus of the NMCA.

The NMCA includes the vast spaces between a handful of provincial parks and wilderness areas, such as Slate Islands Provincial Park, a 6,570-hectare preserve of mature boreal forest located offshore from the town of Terrace Bay. The doughnut-shaped archipelago of islands is separated from the mainland by a ten-kilometre-wide channel and provides predator-free habitat for Ontario's most southerly herd of woodland caribou. The population density of woodland caribou on the Slates is thought to be among the highest in the world, with populations ranging between one hundred and six hundred animals, the number shrinking and expanding in cycles based on browse availability.

With Harper's approval, the federal government is now responsible for working with MNR to finalize boundaries between federal, provincial, and private lands and develop a management plan for the NMCA. Yurick says $36 million has been earmarked for capital development, operations, and maintenance for the next ten years. Meanwhile, the feds and the province are working together to develop the area's first management plan, which will outline its policies and procedures with regards to recreational use and regulations.

The Lake Superior NMCA is not Canada's only marine park. Fathom Five, which started out as a provincial park and joined the federal suite in 1987, protects a portion of Georgian Bay near the tip of the Bruce Peninsula in southern Ontario. But Lake Superior will be the first to put the mettle of the Canada NMCA Act to the test. Revisions to the Fathom Five management plan and guidelines for future NMCAs will follow the blueprint established by the Lake Superior Conservation Area. As a result, Anne Bell, a scientist and policy advisor with the Toronto-based advocacy group Ontario Nature, says it's important to do it right. "We know from a long history of experience that development adjacent to a terrestrial protected area can have devastating impacts on its ecological integrity," says Bell. "I think we can safely assume that this is true of aquatic protected areas as well. It's obvious that development will need to be carefully managed, but what else will it take to adequately protect the water column and the species and natural communities that inhabit it?"

The situation at Paradise Island typifies one of the challenges facing the Lake Superior NMCA. Much of the land that would logically fall within the conservation area is excluded. In most instances, these parcels are Crown (public) land, but some, including Paradise Island, are privately owned. Of the 733 islands contained within its boundaries, 601 are protected. But most islands larger than one hundred hectares are omitted, including St. Ignace Island, which measures over thirty thousand hectares and is home to a remnant herd of woodland caribou. And the vast majority of the mainland does not fall within the jurisdiction of the NMCA.

This means that cottage developers could purchase privately owned land and only be subject to local municipal or provincial regulations. A prime example is a thirty-eight-hectare lot on Vert Island that's for sale and located in Nipigon Bay, within a few kilometres of the public marina in Red Rock.

Brian Christie, the past executive director of the Lake Superior Conservancy and Watershed Council (LSCWC), a non-profit advocacy group based in Sault Ste. Marie, says he could live with some private land development so long as it's "reasonable and done in a manner that's consistent with the management principles of the NMCA. But since [cottages] usually include lawns and gardens, there's an environmental price to pay," he adds, citing concerns of fertilizer-laced runoff entering Lake Superior. "Plus, it's somewhat incongruous with a supposedly wilderness area to come around a bend and be faced with a three-storey log home and all that goes with it."

In theory, Parks Canada can "buy certain private lands if the option becomes available," says Yurick. But these can only be acquired by a "willing seller and willing buyer."

Bob Hartley, a member of the Lake Superior Binational Forum, an international policy advisory group, says that purchasing additional land is less important than drawing up a plan that controls development on coastal Crown land. "There's a dynamic and delicate interaction between land and water on Lake Superior," says Hartley. "If the shoreline land isn't protected, aquatic habitat will be threatened."

Because of Lake Superior's depth and cold water, explains Hartley, the nutrient-rich, life-supporting littoral zone along the shoreline is narrower and more fragile than that of other Great Lakes, making the protection of the coastal corridor all the more important.

The Black Bay Peninsula is a boot-shaped, seventy-five-kilometre-long spit of land stretching into the heart of the Lake Superior NMCA southwest of the town of Red Rock. Entirely undeveloped, it provides the usual mosaic of boreal habitat, including wetlands, recent burns, and a dense forest of black spruce. The peninsula supports thriving populations of moose, black bear, and the odd woodland caribou. But only a handful of parcels of land on the Black Bay Peninsula are protected by the NMCA.

It takes me nearly two days to paddle the thirty-five-kilometre-long "sole" of the peninsula, from Magnet Point to Fluor Island. Enveloped in a fog bank, I grip my paddle with white knuckles and follow my compass, trying to relate the islands I pass with the dozens on my map. I shift my course to northeast when I think I've reached Shesheeb Bay, a ten-kilometre-deep gulch cutting into the midsection of the Black Bay Peninsula. As if on cue, the fog lifts like a stage curtain and reveals the towering red rock cliffs of Otter Island. I follow a five-kilometre-long arm of sheltered water to Otter Cove, where I touch down and follow a chattering stream inland by foot. Soon, I'm swimming in a pool beneath a ten-metre-tall cascade. If it weren't for the mop-topped forest of black spruce, I'd swear I was in the tropics.

Although loggers explored the Black Bay Peninsula sixty years ago, companies preferred to exploit more accessible forests closer to the Trans-Canada Highway. But as timber becomes increasingly scarce, Hartley is concerned that it's only a matter of time before forest access roads weave across the Crown lands of the peninsula. Logging in non-protected areas surrounding the reserve would compromise the NMCA's mandate of protecting the Lake Superior ecosystem, says Hartley. "Crown land along the shoreline and the tributary rivers flowing into Lake Superior need to be protected. If the management plan doesn't control the use of Crown land, how will it be successful in controlling development on private lands?"

Another potential weak spot in the Lake Superior NMCA is a loophole that exempts several marine and coastal areas with "very high mineral potential" from NMCA protection for the next seven years, during which time mining exploration and development would be allowed. Moreover, operating licence-holders could apply for renewal indefinitely after the seven-year window.

A 2001 report commissioned by the Ontario Ministry of Northern Development and Mines identified six sites bordering the NMCA as candidate aggregate resource areas. If a pending deep-water port, quarry, and processing facility goes through on Lake Superior near Wawa, 250 kilometres east of the NMCA boundary, Christie warns that the entire north shore could become a hot spot for aggregate production.

What's more, with uranium trading high on the global market, over six thousand claims encompassing more than one hundred thousand hectares of land have been staked in mainland areas adjacent to the NMCA in a span of only two years. This particular terrain acts as a three-hundred-kilometre-long wildlife corridor linking the NMCA to northwestern Ontario's Wabakimi Provincial Park and the James Bay Lowlands beyond. It also drains into Gapen's Pool on the Nipigon River.

"Mining is one of those activities that has the potential to disrupt recharge areas and groundwater flow, both of which are critical for coaster brook trout," says the MNR's Rob Swainson. "The possibility of contamination is huge if there's any development in the area."

Making a tactful transition from a fickle regional economy dependent on exploiting forests and minerals to one based on sustainable tourism and responsible resource management is the NMCA's key to success, says Hartley. Both Hartley and Parks Canada's Gail Jackson agree that in establishing controls within the reserve and in neighbouring lands, Parks Canada must interact and co-operate with local communities.

"Whether they supported [the NMCA] or not, everyone I spoke to in the task force meetings was really passionate about keeping the area the same," says Jackson. "As the NMCA evolves, we hope to develop partnerships with local communities and turn passion into stewardship."

Much of Lake Superior's north shore remains pristine wilderness. Along the northeastern portion of the lake, Neys Provincial Park, Pukaskwa National Park, Lake Superior Highlands Conservation Reserve, and Lake Superior Provincial Park bookend together to protect a near-continuous four-hundred-kilometre-long swath of coast. In the spring and fall, I've sea-kayaked in these areas for weeks at a time without seeing a soul, let alone a cottage or private property sign. After I first paddled the Silver Islet to Rossport route in 2003, it came as a surprise to find cottages sprouting up at some of my favourite campsites in subsequent years.

After my idyll on Paradise Island, I continue paddling east and set up camp for the next night on a steep cobblestone islet at the southeast corner of St. Ignace Island. Twilight blends water and sky into ever-darkening shades of blue. The feeling of mystery is heightened by the metre-deep dugout depressions known as Pukaskwa Pits that dot the rocky beach. It's thought that teenage Ojibwa once held vision quests at rugged, exposed places like this, fasting and patiently peering out from the pits at the same scene, awaiting hallucinations of

The east-facing cobblestone beach on Spar Island looks out at the Lamb Island lighthouse, Fluor Island, and the south end of the Nipigon Strait, all of which are contained within the Lake Superior National Marine Conservation Area.

the supernatural. But the magic is fleeting, diminished by a cottage — modest by Georgian Bay standards, but development nonetheless — that now stands on a nearby spit of land.

Thankfully, organizations like the LSCWC are promoting public awareness and working to acquire privately owned land within the Lake Superior NMCA and safeguard it from development. Gail Jackson says this approach to stewardship supports her community-based model of management, and, she hopes, will do much to get locals excited about exploring and learning about their watery backyard.

"I envision a great synergy here," says Jackson. "I know we celebrate and share the lake with some great neighbours."

As it happens, the biggest conservation news in northwestern Ontario is coming from the grassroots. In late 2007, the Thunder Bay Field Naturalists garnered the support of the provincial government's Greenlands Program and several private donors to purchase Paradise Island, adding it to their network of nature reserves. Meanwhile, in 2009 the Nature Conservancy of Canada brokered Ontario's largest-ever conservation project by partnering with its sister organization in the United States and the provincial and federal governments to ante up $7.4 million for sizeable Wilson Island and seven smaller islands, just south of Rossport. This nineteen-hundred-hectare cluster — previously open to logging, mining exploration, or cottage development, and off limits to recreational use — is home to endangered species like peregrine falcons and significant communities of Arctic vegetation, as well as First Nations cultural sites. Under the conservation deal, the islands will be protected and openly accessible to paddlers and other outdoor enthusiasts. "It's an amazing landscape," says the Nature Conservancy of Canada's Chris Maher. "This project has been on the conservation community's wish list for many years. The area is one of the most biologically diverse in Ontario."

In good weather it takes only a day to paddle from the east end of St. Ignace Island to the take-out at Rossport. But Lake Superior has a way of mocking the best-laid plans. By lunch, gale-force winds and a heavy swell leaves me stranded on Simpson Island, halfway between the island and the mainland. Jackson is fond of saying that more than any management plan, Lake Superior's ice-cold water, volatile temperament, and largely uninhabitable coastline are its greatest protectors from the damages wrought on the other Great Lakes. I agree with her. Playing castaway, I comb the agate-laced, black stone beach and scramble atop Beetle Point, where geodes cast toothy grins to the sky and encrusted saxifrage — a diminutive, cactus-like succulent of Arctic descent — clings to bare rock. I tuck into a sheltered cleft above the booming waves and drift off, lolled by the timeless rhythm of the restless lake.

CHAPTER 5

Hollowed Bones and Frayed Nerves

The Pukaskwa River flows along the southern boundary of Pukaskwa National Park and feeds into Lake Superior in the middle of a 180-kilometre-long stretch of undeveloped coastline between Marathon and Wawa. The river has a reputation of being one of the most challenging whitewater canoe trips in the Lake Superior basin. First off, there's the guesswork of deciding when to paddle it: Go too early and you'll encounter dangerously high, "pushy" water levels and snow-covered portage trails; go too late and you'll be left dragging your canoe down a bouldery riverbed.

For years, the river went unmaintained by park staff, its portage clogged with deadfall and debris. Paddlers ran the Pukaskwa using a combination of river savvy, whitewater skills, and dogged determination. The only guidebook for the river rated the difficulty of rapids using a bizarre points system in which prospective canoeists' whitewater skills were evaluated based on their ability to perform pushups and various other feats of strength. More recently, a high school outdoors program from the nearby community of Manitouwadge has done wonders in reclaiming the Pukaskwa River's portage trails and making it friendlier for canoe trippers. Still, it remains one of the most difficult trips in Ontario.

Before I canoed it, a friend told me to prepare for an experience that would change my life. The two-week trip down the flooding Pukaskwa River and along the Lake Superior coastline to Michipicoten Bay did just that. My time on the river in May of 2003 pushed the limits of my leadership and canoeing skills in the face of adversity. Besides testing the limits of my endurance, the trip was an emotional rollercoaster — a mix of stress, fear, and exuberance in one of Ontario's greatest wilderness areas.

I've got *fifty feet.* That's the first thing I think as the canoe turns into a submarine and I hit the water, rescue line in one hand, paddle in the other, and flutter-kicking like hell for shore. The line, attached to the stern of the now-overturned canoe, pays out behind me. If I run out of line before I reach the shore, I will have to choose between being keelhauled by the canoe over a waterfall or bidding adieu to our canoe and camping possessions. Unburdened by a swamped canoe, my paddling partner Colin has already swum to an eddy of calm water on the shore. I kick and claw at the water as though our lives depend on it. And being some fifty kilometres from the nearest fringe of civilization, adrenaline and luck could be the only things that save us.

The river is ice-cold, but the waves and whirlpools are subsiding. Out of breath and sputtering, I slither atop a bedrock pillow. I grip terra firma with my sopping wet feet and discover just how close we were to disaster. I only had a few feet to spare on the rescue line. Slowly acknowledging the gravity of our near miss, I carefully pendulum the canoe to shore. Downstream, the river falls into a thundering, misty oblivion. It takes us an hour of deep breathing in the warm mid-May sunshine to summon the courage to get back on the water again.

According to Ojibwa myth, the term "Pukaskwa" describes the act of removing marrow from bone in a hot fire. But while canoeing Pukaskwa National Park's namesake river, my trip-mate Colin Macdonald and I learned that this definition tells only part of the story. There are other ways to be de-marrowed on a two-week expedition along one of Lake Superior's wildest rivers: like stumbling amid blowdowns on a non-existent portage trail, feeling the spray of a dicey whitewater rapid, and turning the canoe into a microscopic eddy scant metres above the precipice of a thundering waterfall. In the end, it was the ice-cold floodwater that hollowed our bones while drawing us powerfully downstream to Lake Superior in an experience that neither of us will forget.

The Pukaskwa River carves a pool-and-drop course through the rugged and remote southern half of Pukaskwa National Park, midway between the northern Ontario towns of Wawa and Marathon. At its source, near Gibson Lake, the river is narrow and creek-like, collecting the water of dozens of similarly sized tributaries. Over the next eighty-odd kilometres, the river picks up steam and features over fifty navigable rapids and countless chutes, cascades, and falls that force all but the most daring whitewater boaters to seek out a dozen rough and obscure portage trails. The Pukaskwa spills into Lake Superior at one of the most isolated places on all of the Great Lakes. Ninety kilometres of wild coastline separates its mouth from roadheads to the north and south.

Fortunately for whitewater paddlers, logging roads just outside of national park boundaries have made the Pukaskwa's headwaters somewhat less remote. Two hours of ruts and washouts circumvents three days of physical pain and suffering on the portage-intensive traditional route to its headwaters via the Trans-Canada Highway and Pokei Creek. Loaded down with two hundred pounds of supplies, we slide our plastic canoe into the Pukaskwa southeast of Jarvey Lake, seventy kilometres from Lake Superior. We've allotted seven days to run the river; on the second week of our trip, we will trace the north shore back to my home in Wawa.

Colin and I were once dorm-mates and friends from the University of Guelph. Born unto a family of canoe-trippers (his father is a noted ethno-geographer who created an impressive map of traditional canoe routes in northeastern Ontario's Temagami district), Colin spent his summers working as a canoe ranger in Algonquin Provincial Park and had extensive whitewater kayaking experience. We hashed out a plan during the winter of Colin's gradu-ating year, deciding that an early-season run down the wild Pukaskwa River would be a good way to ease his transition into the workforce. For me it was the opportunity to tick off another waterway in my goal of paddling all of the rivers flowing into Lake Superior's Canadian shore.

On Day One we thread our way through narrow, rock- and tree-choked rapids, and, more frequently, take our lumps in the tangled shoreline bush when the river's gradient gets too steep for comfort and we're forced to portage. After cursing the boulder gardens, logjams, seemingly impenetrable shoreline alders, and equally profuse deadfall, we call it quits for the day in the middle of a portage after a scant six kilometres of downstream travel. Both of us were expecting the expedition to be a tough one, but at the end of the first day we're exhausted and questioning what we've gotten ourselves into.

The better half of the next day is a continuation of the first, and is spent portaging through leftover snowdrifts to avoid the hazards of paddling the steep and tumultuous river. We are basically hacking our own paths, using a swede saw to clear snags from a barely discernable trail and an axe to blaze trees to facilitate finding the way with our second loads. But by lunch, our toil is rewarded with an ever-widening and more navigable waterway. Deep-water, large-waved rapids give us a taste of why the Pukaskwa is known as one of Ontario's best whitewater rivers. From his seat in the bow, Colin draws the canoe around obstructions while I follow suit with complementary strokes

Colin Macdonald portages along a non-existent trail in the upper reaches of the Pukaskwa River. The river is creek-like, fast-flowing, and often clogged with deadfall in its upper reaches, outside the boundaries of Pukaskwa National Park.

in the stern. We backpaddle to buy time and shout orders back and forth to ferry the canoe to and fro across the current when the going gets tough. Things would be idyllic were it not for the splashes of river that find their way over the gunwales — ice-cold precursors of what's to come.

The heavens open up with monsoon ferocity on Day Three. Wind whips a cold, heavy rain across the river, but once we get on the water, we have little choice but to continue downstream. In a half-day of high-consequence white-water canoeing, we tempt hypothermia, successfully running our first Class III rapid — typically the upper limit of difficulty for open-tripping canoes — and countless other stretches of fast water. By noon we're shivering and wisely decide to stop for the day, pitching camp on an exposed bedrock dome at Lafleur's Dam. We duck under a low-slung tarp and, still clad in lifejackets and whitewater helmets, warm up over a pot of hot soup and tea. Although our tent site is buffeted by strong, gusty winds, it's the only spot that isn't pooling with rainwater. While our shelter weathers the storm admirably, I suspect it has something to do with the two dead weights huddled inside.

When the rain tapers to drizzle a day later, we wander through the wreckage of Lafleur's logging camp. In the grass, we find an old potbellied woodstove and rusty, square-headed spikes. We discover the rundown bunk-house and watch the water pouring over the rotted out sluiceway. The dam itself has long since washed away. Between 1917 and 1930, this place would have been bustling with Scandinavian and Irish loggers who lived here in the winter and spring. Spruce, fir, and the odd white pine were axed, bucked, and dragged to the river's edge by horse. In the spring, at the peak of high water, the dam's floodgates were opened and thousands of cords of wood flushed like matchsticks downstream.

Today, we watch as the river's water level rises disconcertingly quickly. What was bare rock the day before is now buried under a half a metre of frothy, swift-flowing water. The portage around Lafleur's Dam is flooded and we're forced to head inland to find a new launch site, finally deciding on a small cliff where we use ropes and pulleys to lower the fully-laden canoe. On the water, we bump into pieces of driftwood and dodge full-size trees that have been picked up by the freshet. The river feels alive and feral, pulsing, boiling, and making us nervous and edgy.

Between Lafleur's Dam and the next campsite at another derelict logging camp five kilometres downstream, the Pukaskwa flows over several cascades that are rendered more violent by the flood. A portage trail traces the slippery rocks at the river's edge around Slab Rock Falls, a galloping mess of white horses, whirlpool eddies, and powerfully re-circulating hydraulics. Shortly thereafter, we nose into the flooded portage at Boulder Falls. The extremely high water gives us unorthodox alternatives to traditional river tripping: we paddle a slalom course through alder bushes to avoid canoe-eating waves and avoid the pains of portaging. Still, it's like we're tiptoeing on the back of a flame-belching dragon. Red-hot adrenaline rushes through our veins and bone marrow oozes forth.

Day Five begins innocuously enough. We linger at the spectacular campsite at Oxford Ledge, waiting for the sun to dry the dew off the tent and studying the map of the route ahead. Today features the most challenging whitewater: On the topographical map, a series of hash marks, brackets, and contour lines cross the river, indicating four kilometres of continuous rapids and falls. While the water level is starting to stabilize, the river is still flowing frighteningly high.

We successfully run a couple of drops with a combination of vicious back-paddling, shoreline sneak routes, and blind luck. The notion of paddling in reverse to give us time to scout the route and choose a course in a difficult rapid and manoeuvre around tough spots is new to Colin, but we make do and gain confidence along the way. At several points we're forced to hack our own portages through the shoreline bush when what are typically runnable rapids turn into rows of two-metre standing waves. Despite the hardships and the stress of constantly being at high alert, our spirits soar with the blue sky and bright sunshine. Before breaking for lunch, we decide to run a question-able stretch of standing waves and swirling eddies ending barely one hundred metres above a waterfall.

It quickly becomes obvious that our open-decked canoe won't survive this rapid. Time stands still and waves wash over the gunwales one by one in torturous slow motion. The canoe floods, lists to starboard, and turtles. As we abandon ship, I grab the rescue line attached to the stern deck.

Luckily, we've capsized at the end of the wave train and our swim to shore — though bone-chilling — isn't a long one. Colin and I both land on the same granite tongue. After catching our breath, we right the swamped canoe and find all our gear intact. After resting for an hour, we gingerly ferry the canoe across the river to portage the upcoming waterfall. For the rest of the day, paddling the calm water between gut-churning cascades offers brief respite to boot-packing canoe and gear over the most rugged portages we've encountered so far. After a quick dinner in fading late-evening light, it's all we can do to stumble into the tent and fall unconscious for the night.

If every whitewater river has a crux, the Pukaskwa's is Ringham's Gorge. Here the topography goes haywire, funnelling the river over ledges, rapids, and falls and into the rocky abyss of a one-hundred-metre-deep canyon. In low and medium water levels, it's said that skilled whitewater canoeists can paddle the gorge by carefully running rapids and completing short leftovers where necessary. But in high water, Ringham's Gorge is suicidal. The trouble is, the carry around it is equally sketchy.

From our campsite at what's supposed to be the beginning of the portage, we load up with backpacks and wander aimlessly in search of a way through a mass of alders to gain access to the two-and-a-half-kilometre-long trail. At one point, a sizeable pond forces us to dump our load and retrace our steps for the canoe. After we paddle across the giant puddle, the trail becomes easier. We rock-hop up a steep slope and find an old tote road that was built and used by horse loggers eighty years ago and follows a pronounced ridge, affording us occasional views of the canyon below. It takes us about an hour along the rocky remains of the road to reach the river's edge. We spend the better part of the day on the trail, each carrying two back-breaking loads. Back on the water, we're yet again exhausted. What's more, our conversations have become strained, each of us fatigued by the constant mental stresses of the river and lost in our own thoughts. It's all we can do to float downstream in search of a campsite; when we find a suitable spot alongside a stunted waterfall, Colin settles in the tent to write in his journal while I mindlessly tend a fire and restlessly thumb through a novel. Though we never admit it to each other, the river is taking its toll.

After Ringham's, the Pukaskwa meanders a sinuous course, as if gathering strength for its final hurrah. We carefully negotiate a Class III rapid through a small canyon before pulling over for the last portage of the trip within two kilometres of Lake Superior at Schist Falls. For once, portaging is easy. We make

it around in record time and wander back up to admire the river's closing act
— consecutive ten-metre drops beneath towering cliffs of flaking, shiny rock
formations known as schist. Lounging on the rocks at the end of the trail, we
gaze out at the open water of Lake Superior and back at the foaming currents at
the base of the falls. We quietly congratulate each other for surviving the river,
load up, and dip our paddles for our last strokes on the Pukaskwa River.

Just then, like the mist rising from Schist Falls and blending into the thick
bank of fog over Lake Superior, our tensions lift. The challenges of the next
seven days of canoeing on open waters are dwarfed by what we've just accomplished. With ice water flowing through our bones, we know that the best is
left to come.

*The author (left) and Macdonald relax at the mouth of the Pukaskwa River after a strenuous
week of whitewater canoeing on one of the most remote rivers in Ontario.*

CHAPTER 6

The Hard Way

As recently as my late teens I dreamed of being a geologist. My reasons stemmed from romantic notions and youthful innocence. I wanted to be the guy in a plaid jacket, travelling across the north in a cedar canvas canoe in search of mineral riches — and adventure. My favourite canoe, the Chestnut Prospector, *might have had something to do with my career aspirations. Then there was my uncle, a geologist who, with the right provocation, would recount lavish stories of staking claims and exploring the wild Hood River region of the Northwest Territories. For most of the year he lived under canvas and roamed the north, smoking cigarettes to fend off the bugs. I listened carefully when he said the seventeen-foot Grumman was the ultimate canoe for wilderness tripping because it was held together by more rivets than any other brand of aluminum canoe.*

To be sure, the old-time prospectors, like trappers and early loggers, were masters of the bush. Admittedly, I am sure some of the current generation of geologists are equally skilled in the outdoors. But I have a confession to make: it wasn't a newfound awareness of the environmental and social impacts of mining — the ultimate end game of prospecting — that pushed me away from the discipline. It was my ineptitude at math.

Shortly after I was accepted to study geological engineering at the University of Waterloo, I was required to write the Descartes Mathematics Contest, a series of high-level problems in algebra and calculus ostensibly employed by the university to dole out scholarship money. But I know the real reason behind the Descartes test: to scare away hackers like me. I scored a whopping 4 percent on the test, promptly declined Waterloo's offer, and chose to study environmental sciences instead.

While many northern newspapers, websites, and radio stations have championed mining, I like to think I've always written about the industry through a greener lens focused on the broader horizon. Perhaps it's that romanticism that drew me to prospecting as a youth that now makes me think of cratering deep into the carapace of the Earth as despicable. Yet, of course, the inescapable irony is I still use the products of mining in my everyday life. The social and environmental impacts of mining are as undeniable as the pulses of economic stimuli it injects in the north and the truth that all booms will someday bust.

Lake Superior rests in the 1.1-billion-year-old depression left behind when plate tectonics pulled the North American continent apart. Known as the Midcontinent Rift System, this geologically diverse area holds some of the world's greatest mineral deposits. Unlike the lower Great Lakes, whose underlying bedrock has largely been buried beneath the sediments of salt-water seas, magma-borne granites and gabbro intersect with volcanic basalts in the Lake Superior basin, creating lodes of copper, veins of gold, silver, and platinum, pockets of uranium, and copious quantities of iron ore.

Beginning four thousand years ago, Aboriginal people chipped off pieces of exposed copper to fashion tools; this type of benign, subsistence mining is nothing compared to the multi-billion-dollar industry that it has evolved into today. The onslaught of mining claim stakes, razed topsoil, drilled shafts and adits, and crater-like open pits that began in the 1840s in Michigan's Keweenaw Peninsula continues, leaving a legacy of contaminated mounds of waste rock, toxin-laced lakes, acid-killed rivers and forests, poisoned ground-water and soil, and once-booming towns, now abandoned.

The early Copper Country prospectors must have known that they were on to something good — boulders of pure copper could be collected by hand, ready for refining. Between 1855 and 1968, more than 140 processing mills dotted the 240-kilometre-long Keweenaw, which juts into the heart of Lake Superior and whose volcanic geology mirrors that of much of the Canadian shore. Production peaked in the early 1900s, with miners removing upwards of 120,000 metric tonnes of copper per year. Less lucrative nineteenth-century copper-mining operations took place on the Ontario coastline at Coppermine Point, one hundred kilometres north of Sault Ste. Marie, and on isolated Michipicoten Island.

Since copper production in the Keweenaw area slowed in the 1960s, humans have taken stock of the environmental impacts a century of mining has had in the region: 360 million tonnes of copper slurry-like waste products known as "tailings" were sluiced into area waterways; and 60 million tonnes were dumped directly into Lake Superior. W. Charles Kerfoot, a researcher at

Michigan Tech University in Houghton, Michigan, revealed in a 2007 paper that as a result of mining, a toxic "major copper 'halo' exists around the peninsula." What's more, since copper deposits often occur in conjunction with mercury, untold amounts of this neurotoxin also leached into the environment and likely into the food web.

The impacts first hit home in 1987 when the Keweenaw's Torch Lake was declared an Area of Concern under the Great Lakes Water Quality Agreement and a U.S. Environmental Protection Agency Superfund site. With about 20 percent of its capacity filled with mine tailings, the lake was a wasteland: Grotesque tumours "of unknown origin" showed up on fish, vegetation was poisoned by excess dissolved copper concentrations, and benthos populations crashed.

Ironically, there's not one mining company amongst the twenty-six Torch Lake stakeholders listed on the EPA website; like the deposits they exploited, they've all long since vanished. While over $15 million in reclamation funds have regreened the shoreline, biologists estimate that it will be another eight-hundred-plus years before benthic species recover from the high concentrations of metals. In his paper, Kerfoot grossly understated the case of the Keweenaw as "an excellent example of the long-term consequences of mining releases." The same legacy of environmental destruction, social upheaval, and economic boom and bust has played out throughout the Lake Superior basin.

And yet the trend continues. Perhaps the greatest influence on mining in the past decade has been skyrocketing prices of commodities, fuelled by a combination of high demand and increasing scarcity of supply. Gold is a prime example: its price on the London Stock Exchange has increased five-fold since 2000. Meanwhile, an insatiable global demand for so-called "base metals" like nickel and copper has made mining in North America a high-profit industry, despite an otherwise shaky economy.

But as locals take stock of the impacts of rampant mining development, the tide is slowly changing. In Ontario, strong public pressure to overhaul the century-old provincial Mining Act resulted in amendments in 2009. In the same year, a landmark court decision forced mining companies to make public the amount of toxins disposed of in waste materials and atmospheric emissions in Environment Canada's National Pollutant Release Inventory. Most importantly, it is apparent that communities across the Lake Superior basin are standing up for their rights to a healthy environment and long-term social and economic stability in challenging proposed mining developments.

On a sunny, late April day, Catherine Bayne hopscotches her way along a steep and rocky portion of the northeastern shore of Lake Superior. I follow behind, balancing unsteadily on the wave-washed rocks; at the very least, a slip would mean an icy swim. Bayne seems unaware of the danger. Her eyes sparkle in the sunlight as she admires the rugged beauty of the coastline.

"It doesn't take someone with a geology degree to be able to tell that this place is special," says Bayne, who owns 310 hectares of land straddling the Trans-Canada Highway, about one hundred kilometres northwest of Sault Ste. Marie, Ontario. "Just look at all the colours and textures in the shoreline. There are sedimentary, igneous, and metamorphic rocks side by side."

Bayne and her partner, George Browne, live off the grid and telephone-free on a rugged, steep, and rocky piece of northeastern Ontario they call BayNiche Conservancy. Running water comes from a garden hose that diverts some of the flow of a stream and drinking water is scooped from a spring. Their homestead is decidedly rustic and isolated — the nearest neighbour lives nearly ten kilometres away.

BayNiche wasn't always so peaceful. Up until Bayne bought the property in 1986, prospectors had run amok, clear-cutting parts of the land to drill and dig for bedrock samples. The area has been the site of ongoing prospecting and commercial mining activity for more than 160 years. You can still see parts of an 1840 copper mine hidden along the coastline adjacent to Bayne's property, and the sixty-year-old headframe of Canada's first uranium mine stands precariously adjacent to the Lake Superior coast about ten kilometres to the north. Ironically, the saving grace for BayNiche is that since the land is patented, or designated, for mining, Bayne can own both its surface and mineral rights by paying over $1,000 in annual mining taxes. However, if she misses a payment, she forfeits those rights back to the province, thus reopening her land to prospectors. Difficult and stressful as this is on her meagre income as a photographer, it's worth every penny to keep her property free of mining interests.

Rudimentary indigenous copper mines dating back at least four thousand years have been discovered on Michigan's Isle Royale, Lake Superior's largest island, but the real mining rush that continues today in properties abutting

Catherine Bayne spends over $1,000 each year to secure the mineral rights and keep prospectors off of her 310-hectare BayNiche Conservancy on the northeastern shore of Lake Superior.

Bayne's oasis and throughout the basin began on the Keweenaw Peninsula in the 1840s. The region was the world's second-largest producer of copper, producing 4.8 million tonnes between 1850 and 1929.

On the Canadian side of Lake Superior, standoffs between copper miners and local First Nations at Pointe aux Mines, just north of BayNiche, led to the signing of the Robinson-Superior Treaty in 1850, essentially availing much of the rugged north shore to future prospecting. About the same time, four decades of silver mining began at an underground deposit beneath tiny Silver Islet, in the offshore waters of Lake Superior, east of Thunder Bay. Iron mines were developed near Marquette, Michigan, in 1845 and in Minnesota's Mesabi Range in 1882; the region surrounding Lake Superior's westernmost bay still accounts for 75 percent of the United States' production of iron ore.

After several false starts and modest successes in the Marquette area and in northern Ontario's Nipigon and Wawa regions, significant gold deposits were found and exploited in the Hemlo area, south of Marathon, Ontario, in the early 1980s. At their peak, three Hemlo mines produced the lion's share of gold in Canada. Only the multinational Barrick Gold Corporation–operated Williams Mine remains in production today, employing nearly five hundred workers and moving a whopping fifteen hundred tonnes of rock per day. Wesdome's Eagle River Mine and Richmont's Island Gold both operate significant mines just north of Wawa. And closer to Thunder Bay, North American Palladium's Lac Des Iles open-pit mine has produced the platinum group metals used in automobile catalytic converters and other high-tech industries since it was developed in 1993.

The long tradition of mining in the Lake Superior basin shapes the region socially, economically, and politically. There's no doubt that mining brings employment to otherwise economically depressed regions, including high-paying blue-collar and professional jobs. For instance, Ontario's Ministry of Northern Development and Mines (MNDM) reports that in 2009 mineral activity in the province was worth $6.3 billion and provided twenty-three hundred direct jobs. As a result, the MNDM mandate is clear in its priority to put mining activity ahead of environmental and social responsibilities to maintain Ontario's record as a "global mining force."

Despite efforts to modernize mining legislature to encourage public consultation and accommodate the rights of First Nations, policy and industry lags in this regard. In 2001, the North Bay, Ontario-based

Rusty barbed wire and tersely worded signs mark the boundary of the Hemlo gold fields. Of the three original mining operations here, only one remains in operation today.

non-governmental environmental group Northwatch noted that few if any benefits were accrued to local Aboriginal groups from the Hemlo and Eagle River mines. Both encompass traditional Ojibwa territory, yet proponents did not produce impact-benefit agreements for local First Nations. This colonial mindset continues today, particularly south of the border in the case of Marquette's pending Kennecott mine, where London, U.K.-based mining giant Rio Tinto has not addressed local concerns that its proposed mining operations will desecrate Eagle Rock, an Aboriginal spiritual site.

Most of mining's environmental legacy and social impacts come as a result of the archaic and streamlined policies that govern its operations. As a rule, mining policy is pro-development, shaped by powerful industry lobbies that are well represented in government agencies like Ontario's MNDM. Although policies have seen small improvements, a thorough assessment of environmental and social impacts is barely necessary for early exploration work — let alone the final approval of a massive-scale mine.

"The [government] assumes that mining is the best use of land," says Marilyn Crawford, a member of the steering committee Bedford Mining Alert, an advocacy group based near Kingston, Ontario. "This old-fashioned, colonial mindset dates back to when the province was trying to populate the north and mining was done with picks and shovels. Today, it amounts to giving our land away."

It's this Wild West mindset that still affords prospectors "free entry" to probe (and bulldoze) privately owned land in much of northern Ontario for minerals and freed up forty-eight hectares of public land in Michigan's Upper Peninsula for the proposed Kennecott Eagle mine. In the 110-year-old Ontario Mining Act, for example, the role of the lead government mining regulatory agency is to issue land tenure, not to control mining activity. Once land is claimed, the prospector has the exclusive right to explore it for minerals and, in the case of public (Crown) land, the MNDMF has no right to refuse leasing the surface rights should the prospector decide to further explore the mineral potential of a claim. The U.S. General Mining Act (1872) upholds similar archaic rights for miners.

Continuing with the Ontario example, mineral exploration is subject to only minimal environmental regulations. Once land is under lease, companies are not required to submit an exploration plan and are not subject to government inspection. In fact, the rehabilitation of an exploration site isn't mandatory until

A mine claim near Wawa. Claim-staking is the first stage in the mining process. A claim unit measures sixteen hectares and can be staked by anyone in possession of a $25 prospector's licence.

more than one thousand tonnes of subsurface rock is excavated or ten thousand square metres of vegetation and topsoil is removed from a sixteen-hectare claim unit. And even then, standards are flexible. Since companies aren't required to report exploration work, Ontario is littered with an untold number of abandoned exploration sites. New regulations are currently under development, but whether even the "modernized" regime will require rehabilitation of mineral exploration sites is still uncertain.

Meanwhile, Canadian statistics demonstrate that about one in every ten mining claims will advance to the exploration stage, but only about one in one thousand exploration projects will develop into an operating mine (and the claim to mine ratio continues to shrink as exploration increases). This is in large part because of the huge federal and provincial tax incentives for junior mining companies. Effectively, these companies are mining the stock market, often at the expense of environmental quality. Investing in these upstart miners is encouraged by a series of "flow-through" tax breaks including 15 percent federal and 5 percent provincial credits. All told, this makes it far more lucrative to explore for new sources of raw materials rather than conserving or recycling existing supplies.

In the odd instance where a prospect evolves into a full-fledged mine, environmental regulations for development are similar regardless of jurisdiction, with few (if any) opportunities for an independent, cumulative, and long-term review of impacts. In Ontario, a loophole has exempted proposed mines from provincial environmental assessment since 1981. (Now into its fourth extension, the MNDM insists it is developing a streamlined "Class" environmental assessment for mining projects in Ontario.)

In 2008, when I asked MNDM senior lands technician Tony Scarr about the Ontario government's role in making land available to prospectors and miners, he compared the province's responsibilities to those of a real estate agent. "The purpose of the Mining Act is first to encourage prospecting and development and second to protect the environment through rehabilitation," explained Scarr. "The role of the ministry is to issue land tenure, not to carry out exploration or permit mining activities. We look after the conveyance of land from one user to the next." In other words, government is effectively distanced from what mining companies do.

Divisions of power between federal and provincial jurisdiction further complicates the regulatory picture, but also lend important additional scrutiny.

"Triggers" such as the potential to disturb fish habitat invokes the federal Canadian Environmental Assessment Act. Depending on the scope of the project, this could entail a small-scale "screening review," a more comprehensive proponent-led assessment, or, rarely, a rigorous panel review process where independent experts assess more complex or controversial projects. It is important to note that in Canada to date, only panel review EA has had the clout and discretion to dismiss mining projects altogether, in the case of two proposed gold and copper mines in northern British Columbia.

The root of mining's legacy of environmental and social impacts is a lack of critical oversight on the part of decision-makers. A 2007 report by West Coast Environmental Law cuts to the core of the problem: "Once mining exploration has occurred and there is a desire to build a mine, industry pressure is such that it is virtually impossible to prohibit this development in order to respect other land uses and objectives."

The impact of the mining industry is obvious in the town of Wawa, located on the Trans-Canada Highway 230 kilometres north of Sault Ste. Marie and just east of Lake Superior. A brief gold rush first brought miners here in the late 1800s; shortly afterwards, Algoma Ore Division's (AOD) iron mines formed the backbone of the community. The last iron ore was blasted from the earth in 1998, but AOD's legacy remains in the form of a forty-kilometre-long, twenty-thousand-hectare treeless zone — the result of atmospheric sulphur dioxide fallout from the processing of ore into iron. An Ontario Ministry of the Environment (MOE) study showed that soil levels of arsenic, another byproduct of processing, were up to fifty times the MOE guidelines in the area; and the study estimated the risk of cancer to Wawa residents as a result of exposure to arsenic was one hundred times the level used to set provincial standards. (Further studies concluded that because Wawa's soil arsenic was "very insoluble and therefore biologically unavailable," the risk to human health was "very low.")

An even bigger concern is the estimated 650 million tonnes of waste materials generated by the Canadian mining industry each year, including over five hundred thousand tonnes of toxic materials — more than any other industry in Canada. Mining is essentially a waste-management industry, says Joan Kuyek, the former national co-ordinator of the Ottawa-based watchdog

Telemark skiing in the "Fume Kill" north of Wawa, Ontario. The atmospheric fallout of a century of processing iron ore resulted in forty thousand hectares of desolate, rockbound hills and acid-killed lakes.

group MiningWatch Canada. Kuyek's research indicates that for any given ore body, 95 to 99.9995 percent of the raw material mined is discarded — one gram of gold is the product of about one tonne of gold-bearing material, besides the one to three additional tonnes of "waste rock" that must be removed to access the ore and is disposed of in mountainous heaps.

Besides mountains of overburden, chemical- and heavy metal-laced sludge ponds of fine-grained mine waste known as "tailings" comprise about 25 percent of mineral extraction byproducts. These are often contaminated with toxic metals like mercury, lead, cadmium, and arsenic. In the Lake Superior basin, for example, Hemlo's Williams Mine in 2009 disposed of 346,119 kilograms of arsenic, 581,137 kilograms of lead, and 2,157 kilograms of mercury, among other dangerous heavy and base metals, in its waste rock piles and tailings ponds. All this material threatens ground and surface water and aquatic ecosystems and requires advanced engineering to contain. Yet the fact remains that impoundment facilities occasionally fail, with two being breached in Canada in 2008.

Tailings storage areas have huge ecological footprints. When it closed in 1996, the White Pine Mine in Michigan's Ontanogan County, east of the Keweenaw Peninsula, seventy years of mining had produced a sprawling 2,630-hectare field of dry tailings from copper-mining operations. Wind erosion caused regular "dust storms" of tailings that impacted nearby communities, and the estimated cost of "capping" the impoundment area with a layer of clay was pegged at US$72 million. Today, the site is re-vegetated with hardy plant species after two years of research and reclamation work by the University of Montana and ongoing maintenance. Yet questions remain about the subsequent uptake of metals by plants that could flow upwards into the food chain.

Furthermore, since most contemporary mining in the Lake Superior basin occurs in sulphur-bearing rock, there's an elevated risk of waste rock and tailings developing acid mine drainage and metal leaching. These interconnected chemical processes occur when subsurface, sulphur-bearing materials are exposed to and react with water and air, creating sulphuric acid. Because dangerous metals like lead, zinc, copper, and mercury become more soluble in acidic conditions, a positive feedback loop develops where increasingly acidic mine runoff becomes laced with higher and higher concentrations of toxins. Paradoxically, acid mine drainage does not necessarily occur immediately and may take years, decades, or even centuries to develop. Abandoned mine sites like Wawa's George W. MacLeod mine are ticking time bombs: Once water levels in open pits and craters hit a certain point, the production of sulphuric acid and the leaching of dangerous metals can occur. Two abandoned Noranda Minerals Inc.-owned mines near Manitouwadge, Ontario, will generate acidic, heavy-metal-contaminated runoff in perpetuity.

Leaching of arsenic, selenium, and molybdenum can also occur in neutral and alkaline conditions. Needless to say, the costs of dealing with such challenges are steep, and the need for monitoring is perpetual. At the closed White Pine Mine in Ontonogan, underground mining released mineral-laced groundwater into surface water, with Mineral River, a Lake Superior tributary, containing ten times the concentration of dissolved solids as seawater. A 2009 Lake Superior Binational Forum report indicated that in fifty years, the Mineral River would not be able to support life and a four-hectare area at its mouth on Lake Superior would reach "chronic toxicity."

With Canadian mines using upwards of 2 billion cubic metres of water per year, it's no surprise that MNDM case studies demonstrate that 70 percent of operations contaminate surface water and 65 percent pollute groundwater. Finally, there's the footprint of the mine itself — the open pits, underground shafts, mounds of waste rock, and sprawling tailing ponds that obliterate habitat,

Mountainous piles of waste rock tower above ore extraction facilities in the Hemlo gold fields, south of Marathon. The typical mine produces two to four tonnes of waste material for every gram of gold.

not to mention the roads and hydro transmission corridors necessary to service the site. In the case of Stillwater Canada's proposed platinum-group mine in Marathon, operations would include an open pit larger that the town site itself; a waste rock pile twenty-seven stories tall; and the rerouting of thirteen watercourses with a series of dams to contain discarded tailings — all in what was once a relatively pristine tract of boreal forest.

Among the most concerning trends in mining today is industry's desire to use natural lakes and waterways for storing tailings. This practice is by no means new — it was the approach favoured by old-time miners like those in the Keweenaw, who dumped the wastes of copper mining into the waters of Torch Lake and Lake Superior. What's scary is a 2002 addition to Canada's Fisheries Act that could resurrect this archaic strategy, making it legally possible to reclassify lakes, wetlands, and waterways as "tailings impoundment areas." Were it not for the quick, tactful action of a group of concerned citizens, Ontario's first lake to be sacrificed by this provision would've been just north of Lake Superior.

Sometimes environmental controversy spurs even the most reticent citizens to action. Soft-spoken Ted Schintz says he was "indignant" when he caught wind of a proposal to fill a healthy cold-water lake with toxic mining byproducts near his hometown of Marathon, in northern Ontario.

The Toronto-based proponent of the platinum, palladium, and copper mine, which has since been absorbed by Stillwater Canada, wanted to dump over 60 million cubic metres of tailings into pristine Bamoos Lake, which drains into Lake Superior, over eleven years of mining. As compensation, it promised to rehabilitate the storage area for warm-water fish species once ore deposits ran dry. "I couldn't believe it," says Schintz, who's lived on the north shore of Lake Superior since the 1970s. "There's something wrong if someone is allowed to take away a deep, cold lake capable of supporting trout in favour of a shallow, polluted pike pond."

But Schintz was daunted by the prospect of speaking out against a mine that promised much-needed jobs for his community, which is suffering from chronic unemployment in the wake the 2009 closure of a pulp-and-paper mill. "For a while, I thought, 'What am I going to do?'" he says. "But then someone else mentioned that they were not happy with the situation, either. That got the ball rolling."

Schintz, along with fellow Marathon residents Michael Butler and Teri Burgess, and Bonnie Couchie, a friend from nearby Pic River First Nation, formed Citizens for a Responsible Mine (CRM) in the spring of 2010. They turned to MiningWatch Canada program coordinator Ramsey Hart for a crash course in mining policy, started a blog, and shared their message with people in the community. Their Facebook site racked up hundreds of supporters locally and around the world. All the while, they took the unusual tack of stressing their support for mining; they knew it would be suicidal to be in outright opposition of development. "We decided that if we didn't define who we were, someone else would do it for us," Schintz recalls. "Quite often and quite early we said that we supported the mine, but we didn't support irresponsible mining activities."

CRM focused on tactfully engaging the mine proponent and bringing out facts about mining's tarnished history, such the precedent-setting implications of turning a healthy lake into a tailings pond and the importance of properly funded mine closure plans. "Until we got involved, the narrative was tightly controlled by the proponent," says Butler, a fisheries biologist. "Bits of corporate spin were being printed verbatim by the newspaper. What we were able to do is present a counterbalance to that corporate message. It became a public dialogue instead of them controlling the message."

Even though CRM's campaign galvanized local support, it came as a surprise to everyone when the proponent suddenly shelved the Bamoos plan in July 2010. In a press release, vice-president of operations Raymond Mason said, "After consultation with First Nations, government agencies and residents of Marathon and surrounding communities, it became clear that the loss of the fishery in Bamoos Lake was undesirable."

For Schintz and his colleagues, it was a "great victory" that brought them one step closer to creating something the mining industry has yet to achieve: a carefully planned mine that imposes the least possible environmental impact, respects regulations, and doesn't hold taxpayers accountable for costly, long-term, government-led cleanups once production ceases. "There's no such thing as a 'model mine' in Ontario," says CRM's Butler. "Hopefully, the example we set here will be one that, even [in a depressed economy], [will provide] an opportunity for people to speak up to make sure that environmental concerns are taken into account."

• • •

The economic benefits of mining — in the short term, at least — are clear. With so much money to be made, investors and government agencies have been quick to support the industry. But while stock market figures steadily rise, the tide is slowly changing in the communities that host mining developments. A 2001 Northwatch report identified examples of the social impacts of mines: The incidence of silicosis, a deadly lung ailment due to exposure to silica-bearing rock dust, in Hemlo miners; the lack of impact-benefit agreements between First Nations and mining companies in the Hemlo and Wawa gold fields; and the threat of arsenic-poisoned soil in the vicinity of Algoma Ore Division's abandoned Wawa sinter operations.

These concerns remain strong today in mining communities, along with new revelations of the perils of sinking all hope in what is essentially a temporary industry — not to mention a growing resentment toward the adverse effects resource extraction has on sustainable industries like tourism. In spite of governments' inability to fully grasp the perpetual impacts of mining on the environment, the example of Marathon demonstrates that communities have become more wary of promises of short-term jobs and prosperity.

More hard-hitting is the reality that the future of mining promises fewer and fewer jobs as large-scale multinationals seek to minimize costs through automation and new technology. These trends are already well underway. According to the Lake Superior Binational Program, the workforce in Minnesota iron mines has decreased by 83 percent since 1979. This product of increased technology has done little to settle the volatile, boom-bust economy of mining communities.

Rio Tinto, the same company promising plenty of nickel-mining jobs at its Kennecott Eagle mine in northern Michigan, touts robotic mining as the industry's future. According to its website, mines will one day be managed and operated from remote office complexes, rendering the traditional blue-collar role of miners obsolete. Rio Tinto's trademarked "Mine of the Future" is already being piloted in Australia. According to the company, the industry's future is "unprecedented levels in automation," with "some of the roles currently based at the mine site ... based in a city thousands of kilometres away." Ironically, it's foreseeable that local ore bodies will be fully exploited and the tourism industry long since vanished due to environmental degradation by the time residents of the Lake Superior basin get to experience the future of mining.

Of the many insights revealed by 150 years of mining in the Lake Superior basin, three general trends stand out: the oft-touted economic benefits rarely match environmental and social impacts; government policy and decision-making protocols highly favour development; and, ultimately, if the objectives of international accords like the Great Lakes Water Quality Agreement are to be met, the premise and practices of mining require critical updates. With the next wave of mining poised to begin operations on all sides of Lake Superior's perimeter and intense exploration suggesting more developments to come, it is imperative to address these issues immediately.

Pressure is mounting on governments to rethink their attitudes toward mines. In Michigan, the Chippewa Ottawa Resource Authority (CORA) has offered compelling arguments to make minimizing mining-related threats a key component to the binational Lake Superior Lakewide Management Plan. Indeed, it is critical to assess the impacts and benefits of mining in the Lake Superior basin from a variety of angles — including achieving the international objectives of the Great Lakes Water Quality Agreement and upholding Lake Superior Zero Discharge Demonstration Program, an ambitious international effort aiming to eliminate the release of harmful contaminants like mercury into Lake Superior altogether. To this end, CORA suggests the concept of smaller-scale, "micro-mining" projects that yield fewer environmental impacts and "longer and more sustained benefits" to communities. Since most contemporary mining proposals involve potentially acid-generating sulphurous rock, small, underground mines could be the best way to contain overall impacts.

In Ontario, provincial environmental commissioner Gord Miller has repeatedly highlighted the need for mining legislation reform in his annual "watchdog" report of environmental policies and practice. For too long, mining exploration and development have only been subject to a piecemeal, uncoordinated review by various government agencies and exempt from comprehensive provincial environmental assessments altogether. "Once mine exploration has occurred, and there is a desire to build a mine, industry pressure is such that it is virtually impossible to prohibit this development in order to respect other land uses and objectives," notes Miller, highlighting a trend that's pervasive on either side of the Canada–United States border.

A key to more responsible decision-making that's been suggested by Miller, MiningWatch Canada, and many other environmental organization is the need for comprehensive assessments that take all impacts and benefits — present and future — into account. Alarming elements are common in all of the current generation of mining proposals. In the case of Kennecott Eagle's proposed Marquette mine, these include habitat impacts to endangered species of flora and fauna, the potential for long-term acid mine drainage, impacts to the local tourism industry, and the destruction of a sacred site to local First Nations. While each of these negative impacts can be mitigated individually with various degrees of certainty, the project is clearly a juggling act when taken as a whole.

The power of coordinated, all-encompassing, independent review is clear in the case of the Canada Environmental Assessment Act's panel review approach to assessing the impacts of a proposed mine. In the fall of 2010, a panel of independent experts rejected Taseko Mines' Prosperity project in Williams Lake, British Columbia, arguing that its "significant environmental effects" could not be justified. Critics agree that it is this kind of unbiased assessment that yields appropriate decisions.

Meanwhile, mining activities continue and the environmental legacy of today's mines will likely befall future generations until developers own up to the full, decades- or even centuries-long costs of mining. The current trend of mining giants creating sacrificial subsidiaries (such as Kennecott, which is a division of Rio Tinto) and "mining the market" for banks, brokers, fund managers, and individual investors means that even large companies aren't required to use their own money to finance a project. This could lead to trouble in the future, when deposits in Marathon and Marquette dry up and mining giants claim innocence from their faraway head offices.

But there's hope to be drawn from the success of Schintz's Marathon group that managed to catch the ear of mining proponents and demonstrate that, sometimes, locals have the capacity to instigate change in their communities. It's this prospect of a capacity for locals to instigate change that rural property owners, concerned citizens, and advocacy leaders like Catherine Bayne, Marilyn Crawford, and Joan Kuyek cling to.

After his first crack at environmental activism, Marathon's Ted Schintz is eager to stay involved. "Now that I've been drawn in, enjoyed some success and made some good friends, I'm more encouraged to take on something again in the future or lend my support to a cause elsewhere," he says.

As the knowledge that all that glitters isn't gold strikes closer to home, so does the time when we can finally stand up for the rights of the land beneath our feet.

CHAPTER 7

The New Voyageurs

Among my friends at Naturally Superior Adventures, a Wawa-based outfitter that offers accommodations, paddling instruction, and guided trips on Lake Superior, is a decade-old rite of passage known as the "Rock to Rock Challenge." Simply put, the challenge involves paddling non-stop from Naturally Superior's Rock Island base, at the mouth of the Michipicoten River, to Agawa Rock, at the south end of Lake Superior Provincial Park. Depending on the route, the distance ranges from seventy-five to one hundred kilometres — an impressive feat for any paddler.

To date, the challenge has been completed four times, and I'm the only one who has participated in each attempt. (Some may say this is a sure sign of low intelligence or a ridiculously high threshold for suffering, or some combination of the two.) Time of passage has ranged from twelve to seventeen hours, depending on weather conditions and group morale. One caveat of the challenge is that it must involve some night paddling — an element that can make or break the expedition. I remember finishing up the graveyard shift on a Rock to Rock mission with my friend David Wells, paddling in a tense silence, fighting hard to stay awake and slogging forwards at half our usual speed. There's nothing more exhausting than paddling at sunrise after spending an entire night on the water. Afterward, we each said that we had our doubts that either of us would come to each other's rescue if one of us had capsized. That epic ended with a four-hour, trance-like sleep on melon-sized boulders on an island near the Ojibwa pictographs at Agawa Rock.

Only once have we tried paddling a variation of the Rock to Rock Challenge as a group in Naturally Superior's thirty-six-foot replica of a voyageur canoe. Though unsuccessful, this attempt revealed insights into the workings of group dynamics and clearly illustrated the strength and stamina of the voyageurs — the French-Canadian "engines of the fur trade" who plied these water two centuries ago. It seems like we spent more time bickering over gear packing lists and nattering about when to take a break than actually paddling. But then again, I've never felt more a part of a community of modern-day voyageurs than on the night thirteen of us bivouacked underneath the voyageur canoe at Old Woman Bay, passing around a bottle of booze and witnessing the colourful history of the fur trade on Lake Superior first-hand.

Days are long as the night is short on Lake Superior in June. Still, darkness had already fallen by the time we landed on the beach at Old Woman Bay, flipped over our thirty-six-foot canoe, and scarfed down a scant dinner — my second of the day — of cold beans and stale pita bread. Now, the first of my voyageur crewmates are snoring restlessly and after a last slug of Irish cream liqueur, I'll join them. In a couple of hours — well before dawn — we'll be back at the paddle.

To settle a debate among paddling friends at Naturally Superior Adventures, an ecotourism outfitter located near Wawa, Ontario, we gathered thirteen voyageur wannabes and piled into a fibreglass replica of a fur-trade canoe to paddle part of the historic trade route along the coast of Lake Superior Provincial Park, which protects a 120-kilometre-long swath of Lake Superior coast from Agawa Bay to Michipicoten Bay, near Wawa.

Sea kayaker Ray Boucher gazes up at the Ojibwa pictographs at Agawa Rock, near Agawa Bay. In 2011, Boucher and the author completed the Rock to Rock Challenge, an eighty-five-kilometre, single-day trip along the Lake Superior Provincial Park, in just under thirteen hours.

This coastal corridor is made up of sand beaches and sheer cliffs, like the ones visible from the Trans-Canada Highway at the popular picnic areas of Katherine Cove and Old Woman Bay. Besides the odd picnic spot, it's undeveloped in its entirety, and, for the most part, separated from the highway by kilometres of boreal bush and surging rivers. It's a pleasant and relaxing five- to seven-day sea kayak or canoe trip for intermediate paddlers.

But we're not looking for this sort of rejuvenating wilderness experience. We're trying to match the pace of the voyageurs, the French-Canadian canoemen of two hundred years gone by, who'd often paddle the entire Agawa-to-Michipicoten stretch in a single sitting as a part of their summer-long, 3,600-kilometre round trip from Montreal's Lachine Canal to Fort William, at the western terminus of Lake Superior. We would head northwest for eighty kilometres, a typical voyageur day, finishing at the mouth of the Michipicoten River where the remains of a fur-trade post that once meant a day or two of rest and high wine for the voyageurs can still be found amid shoreline alders. We thought that after twelve hours of paddling we'd better understand the day-to-day routine of the engines of the Canadian fur trade. What's more, it seemed like a worthy way to celebrate the coming of summer under the full moon of the June solstice.

Before taking our first strokes, however, we have to deal with the challenge of organizing a bunch of free-spirited adventure leaders for a day together on the water. Whereas, individually, each member of our crew is a mature, responsible, and skilled sea-kayak or canoe guide, capable of maintaining a precise schedule while leading groups of beginners on multi-day trips through the largest freshwater lake in the world, taken together we amount to a headstrong beast with multiple brains and no outright decision-maker. Preparation for a simple day trip devolves into a scene of organized confusion. It takes us hours to sort gear, load the canoe, pack the paddles and personal flotation devices, and figure out what we'll eat. Everyone has their own idea of how to do it right. Consequently, it's pushing dinnertime when we finally unload the canoe at Coldwater Creek and drag over a sandbar to Lake Superior, a full twelve hours behind the usual pace of the voyageurs.

Our craft is a modern-day replica of the voyageurs' birchbark *canot du maître*. The fur-trading North West Company discovered that these thirty-six-foot monsters were the ideal way to transport loads on big rivers like the Ottawa, Mattawa, and French, and the open waters of Great Lakes Huron

The thirty-six-foot canot du maître, *or Montreal canoe, was traditionally propelled by ten voyageurs. Unlike this fibreglass replica, the original birchbark voyageur canoes did not have seats; they were designed to maximize capacity of furs and trade goods.*

and Superior. A high bow and stern make it seaworthy in large rapids and ocean-like Great Lakes swells, yet its shallow draft let its crews of voyageurs find protection from sudden gales in the shallowest of coves. At six hundred pounds, it was light enough to be carried over portages by voyageurs glad to get a break from paddling. A key selling point for shrewd North West Company brass in Montreal was the fact that running a fleet of sixty-odd *canots du maître* each summer was the economic equivalent of not piling all your eggs in one basket — or all your furs in one sailing ship: If one canoe went down, only a negligible amount of furs or trade goods would be lost.

Two hundred years ago, dozens of these canoes paddled this shoreline every year, each loaded down with four tonnes of such trade goods as rifles, ammunition, and cooking pots. At Fort William, west of present-day Thunder Bay, the Montreal brigades would rendezvous with a fleet of twenty-six-foot *canots du nord*, each packed to the gunwales with furs from the nearly endless waterways and many fur-trading posts of the Canadian interior.

One hell of a party ensued at the Great Rendezvous, which took place each summer in early July. This was followed by a hasty, hungover exchange of cargo. The canoes then retraced their routes — the *canots du maître* returned to Montreal so the furs could be shipped to Europe, and the *canots du nord* headed back across thirteen-kilometre-long Grand Portage and into the tangled lakes and rivers of the Canadian frontier to stock the trading posts scattered throughout the interior.

It only takes a few minutes on board to realize that paddling a voyageur canoe is like riding in a school bus. They are about the same length and equally unwieldy to steer, and both encourage the same sort of sing-along songs and juvenile humour. In the bow, the *avant* sets the pace in stroke and song and rows of bench seats segregate the *milieu*, which inevitably is comprised of gung-ho paddle pushers in the front and badass lily-dippers in the back. Getting ten to fourteen paddlers in synch is about as easy as keeping a bus-load of grade-schoolers quiet, but when it happens, the canoe cruises along at ten kilometres per hour.

Among the voyageurs, there were no lily-dippers. They paddled sixty-five strokes per minute for eighteen hours a day and were paid a pittance in company credit. They timed their days based on hasty pipe breaks that occurred roughly once per hour. On the portage, bets were wagered over how much weight a man could carry — two ninety-pound bundles were considered the minimum load. Once ashore for the night, respite came in the form of a chunk of pork lard or beans, a slug of gut-rotting high wine, some stale tobacco, and too little sleep on a cold beach, more often than not sheltered from the elements (but not the merciless biting insects) beneath the overturned canoe. It's no surprise that most voyageurs walked with a hunchbacked spine and many died young of a hernia or heart attack on some remote portage.

Meanwhile, our crew of modern voyageurs has barely put on the water and rounded the Baldhead — a pronounced, round-topped headland whose name dates back to the fur-trading days — when someone decides it's time to eat. Our pace slows to a crawl while Vince, our chef and token French-Canadian paddler, sets up a propane stove to heat up a massive pot of baked beans from his *grandmère*'s own recipe. Then we drift and eat, engaged in heated conversation and oblivious to the fact that in taking an hour-long supper break we're burning daylight fast.

Back at the paddles, hardly another hour goes by before someone calls for a shore stop at Gargantua. It was here that the voyageurs saw the parallels between the Ojibwa trickster and demi-god Nanaboozho and King Gargantua, a jovial character of the sixteenth-century French writer Rabelais. We're feeling gregarious ourselves, and what was supposed to be a brief bathroom break erupts into a spirited hula-hoop session on a gravel beach and a spontaneous satellite phone call home for our New Zealander crew member.

It's here that I'm given the role of *gouvernail*, the sternsman responsible for charting the big canoe's course. Still less than halfway to Michipicoten, I decide to take us offshore, crossing ten kilometres of open water from Gargantua to Grindstone Point, just as the voyageurs would've done it two centuries ago. Controlling the canoe's unwieldy momentum requires prying my two-metre-long ash paddle off the gunwale — sometimes a little too much. Too often I find myself over-correcting and causing the canoe to track a meandering course. But the crew has finally settled into a paddling rhythm, I quickly get the hang of steering, and the canoe surges across the glassy, calm water.

Sunset finds us several kilometres offshore and squinting toward the horizon, looking for the cliff-lined entrance of Old Woman Bay. The voyageurs called the unpredictable winds of Lake Superior *La Vielle* — the Old Woman — so it's apt that we encounter southeasterly gusts and choppy waves as we approach the deep, horseshoe-shaped bay. The wind hits the boat at a diagonal

The purpose of the sweeping bow and stern of a voyageur canoe was twofold: to improve seaworthiness in large Great Lakes swells, and to increase headroom underneath when the canoe was overturned on shore. Equipped with only a tarp, the voyageurs spent short nights sleeping beneath their canoe.

and a metre-high chop has us fishtailing even more than usual. It's all I can do to lever the canoe back on course before we wallow and spin out again.

All singing on this bus has ceased by the time darkness falls. With it comes the realization that we're still twenty-five kilometres from Michipicoten and faced with uncertain weather. Old Woman Bay is our last possible pullout.

It seems like I'm the only one arguing in favour of pressing on, but despite my position in the stern of the canoe I'm easily outnumbered. There's no doubt that the voyageurs would've paddled on in these kinds of conditions. Indeed, other than weaving a bit the canoe is running dry and feels every bit at home in the wind and waves. But after fifty-five kilometres of paddling the group is lagging — despite all of the high-energy designer snacks we've consumed. All is quiet except for the howling wind until someone offers a carefully formed argument for calling it a night.

Despite a few half-hearted objections, we decide to head for Old Woman Bay's sweeping crescent-shaped beach. Upon crashing ashore we haul the canoe beyond Lake Superior's reach, flip it over, and curl up underneath. Someone muses how strange our late-night, ghost-brigade arrival must appear to bleary-eyed motorists on the highway.

Our challenge has ended in defeat. But as we find space to sleep with our heads under the overturned canoe I'm startled to look around and see a group of weary, wet, and hungry paddlers looking more like voyageurs than I thought was possible. What began as an organizational debacle and certainly had its low points along the way has somehow morphed into a bonding experience that none of us will ever forget. The only thing that's missing is the pork lard.

While the crew dozes off one by one, a few of us silently pass around a bottle of Bailey's. The sweet liqueur goes down smooth, and, for a fleeting moment, I stare out at the lake and think I catch a glimpse of a big canoe still battling the wind and waves. Someone whispers that they just heard a faint song in the distance. But then, after a quick tip of the bottle it's all lost in the inky darkness and restless wind.

CHAPTER 8

Secrets of the Sauna

The hidden saunas of northwestern Lake Superior's island chain became more than just obscure, second-hand notes on my map the first time I sea-kayaked in the area in the spring of 2004. It was early in the season — ice chunks still clung to many of the rocky headlands — and saunas were a key survival strategy for me and my paddling friend Dave Patterson. The only wild card was that we weren't exactly sure of their locations. But if there's ever someone to embark with on a sketchy adventure on the fringes of paddling season, Dave is your guy.

Dave's good sense of humour and patience paid off on our second day when we combed the shoreline aimlessly for a sauna I had marked on my chart in Squaw Bay on St. Ignace Island. It was foggy, the lake still hovering around the freezing mark and the air temperature not much warmer. Squaw Bay is a beautiful place — a red gravel beach fringed by a boreal forest of spruce and fir — but decidedly missing in one key regard: a sauna. Exhausted after paddling close to fifty kilometres that day, chilled by the cold and acutely aware that sundown was fast approaching, Dave and I were in a bad way.

"Let's paddle just a little bit farther," I implored. Luckily, Dave agreed. His sleeping bag was saturated from the previous night's deluge and all he wanted was a little warmth. A few kilometres down the shore we found CPR Slip, a public sauna and cabin located in a small, hook-shaped cove that's locally known as Squaw Harbour. The chilled air and our sore muscles perfectly complemented the humid heat of one of the nicest steam baths on Lake Superior's north shore.

Since that first trip, which also included a protracted two-night stop at the more secluded, somewhat ramshackle sauna on Swede Island, I've made regular spring outings on the paddling route between the village of Rossport and the Sibley Peninsula. Once, confident in my paddling fitness after a winter spent on the water of Canada's west coast, I made the trip without a tent, relying instead on the secret saunas and their associated cabins for shelter. There is something special about a place where such structures are allowed to persist without graffiti or vandalism, free for all to enjoy.

. . .

The Finnish Sauna Society, a cultural association with 3,500 members created in 1937 to celebrate and preserve the traditions of the steam bath, says *loyly* is the spirit of the sauna. It's the humid, steamy heat that rises from moistened sauna stones when the stove burns hot and the tang of damp cedar emanates from the steam-bath walls. In our effort to re-create a true sauna experience on the north shore of Lake Superior, my paddling buddy Dave and I are looking for maximum *loyly*.

We put forth our best effort to capture the essence of the sauna at Swede Island, an apostrophe-shaped chunk of land located midway along the island-dotted, 125-kilometre-long stretch of offshore waters between the tip of the Sleeping Giant, near Thunder Bay, west to the village of Rossport. I'm doing fine until we douse the stones on the dented and worn sauna stove for the third time. Seventy degrees Celsius of *loyly* sears my eyeballs, tightens my lungs, and leaves me feeling woozy. The instant blast of heat is unbearable. I feel my heart thumping in my neck and temples.

"Run to the lake?" I gasp. It's not so much a question as it is a plea. I'm not a Finn, but neither is my friend Dave. He's out the door almost before the question leaves my mouth and I'm right behind him. I watch his sweaty, naked body hurdle our two sea kayaks with Olympic grace. Soon we're yelping in ice-cold, Lake Superior-in-May water.

But the torture is addictive. Shortly — it may have something to do with the two-degree lake water that could well have been ice the week before — we're back in the sauna, hooked on *loyly* like junkies on crystal meth. "According to Finnish lore," I tell Dave, "if a sauna, liquor, and tobacco don't help you, your condition is fatal."

"I'd take the first two and trade the smokes for a couple of Scandinavian supermodels," he replies. We douse the rocks again and again, and run naked and screaming to the lake a couple more times before calling it a night.

I was two weeks into a spring solo sea-kayaking expedition from Wawa to Thunder Bay when Dave met me in Rossport to join me on the final week of the trip. I was craving fresh food — especially vegetables, fats, and sweet treats — as much as the companionship of a good friend after subsisting on

The old sauna was still there when Thunder Bay native Roger Bailey and friends rebuilt the cabin at an abandoned mining claim on Swede Island, in the Lake Superior National Marine Conservation Area. The building remains as a "safe haven" for mariners in need, although low water levels in recent years have made it more suitable for kayaks than pleasure boats.

carefully measured rations of rice, dried beans, vegetables, and the odd apple for the first leg of my trip. Spring was late to arrive and each day I bundled up in my drysuit and paddled like hell to keep warm. I dared not stop because the temptation to retreat into my tent and sleeping bag with a good book often outweighed any desire to get back on the icy water.

Dave showed up with an eclectic mix of foodstuffs, including hot dogs (which were consumed eagerly after a brief roasting over a campfire — this despite the fact that I was a devout vegetarian at the time), various extra-salty soup mixes to be blended hodge-podge with an assortment of potato flakes and dried vegetables, and bulk food store treasures like chocolate-covered raisins, honey-roasted sunflower seeds, and dates that we would carefully mix each morning as our daily allotment. Curiously missing were the crisp greens and juicy grapefruit I desired the most. But Dave's indefatigable sense of humour easily made up for his culinary omissions.

Between our meeting point in Rossport and our destination of Thunder Bay, the north shore of Lake Superior juts out in a series of sizeable islands, massive peninsulas, and progressively smaller offshore islets. Boxy Simpson Island and the sprawling crescent-shaped and semi-mountainous interior of St. Ignace Island, the largest island on Lake Superior's Canadian shore, lead to the boot-shaped Black Bay Peninsula and eventually the Sibley Peninsula, which in profile takes the form of an eight-kilometre-long, three hundred-metre-tall sleeping giant. In between there are hundreds of small- to medium-sized islands — a paddler's paradise similar to Georgian Bay's Thirty Thousand Islands region or British Columbia's Gulf Island archipelago except the open-water crossings tend to be longer and more difficult, the water icy cold all summer, and the coastline rock- and cliff-bound and far less forgiving. For the most part, the area is too isolated and rugged for pleasure boaters and cottagers; derelict fishing camps and stalwart lighthouses replace obnoxious cigar boats, racing ferries, and multi-million-dollar summer homes.

In embarking on this trip, it wasn't necessarily wilderness sea-kayaking, but rather the siren call of the secret saunas scattered along the way that was most appealing to Dave and me. When we met in Rossport, we swapped my solo tent for a two-person shelter and I waited patiently while Dave loaded his kayak in the parking lot of the public beach. Then we launched, winding our way through Channel and Wilson islands, crossing to Harry Island for lunch, and then ending the day at Battle Island, where a stout lighthouse marks the entrance to the Rossport archipelago. A van-sized chunk of ice still clung to the black basalt pillar atop which the beacon stood and blasted a beam of light across the lonely lake all hours of the day. The place was deserted, the cheery red-and-white painted lightkeepers' residences locked tight.

Then came the rain. Dave somehow managed to turn most of his clothes into sponges before the night was through and the next day we were dead set on making it to the safe harbour at CPR Slip, a public sauna and anchorage about fifty kilometres west. Located on the southwestern side of St. Ignace Island, it would be the first stop on our sauna tour. Getting there meant a long day of cold, wet misery — even worse than the two weeks of steady rain and sleet I'd already endured. Had we taken the time to admire the shore, we would have noticed bizarre, honeycomb-shaped pillars of basalt on Simpson Island's west side, a unique volcanic rock formation similar to Ireland's famed Giant's Causeway, spectacular sea caves and arches, and a handful of undeveloped cobblestone beach campsites along the way.

Instead, our paddle became a death march. Out of shape and not yet accustomed to the cold weather, Dave was exhausted by lunch. I urged him on, insisting that the sauna was just around the next point. We finally arrived at CPR Slip somewhere between the slate-grey skies of twilight and pitch black-ness — on this day there was no sunset. The Canadian Pacific Railway shaped a small harbour and built a retreat for its executives here in the 1930s. After it was abandoned, area pleasure boaters (and no doubt Finns) resurrected the four-bunk cabin and built one of the best saunas on the north shore. It's well-sealed with a powerful, wood-fired stove, concrete floor, and two-tier seating; and, as an added bonus, it's within a fifteen-metre sprint from a prime deep-water jumping place off the dock. At CPR Slip, along with the other saunas of the north shore, good etiquette says you replace any wood you use and leave the place cleaner than you found it.

We enjoyed a good session in the sauna and a well-earned night's sleep on the saggy mattresses of the old camp before taking the most of the morning to dry Dave's gear and recuperate. Beyond CPR Slip, good campsites are a dime a dozen on Fluor Island's southeast shore. We tented out on our third night on Spar Island at the mouth of the Nipigon Straits, gazing across to the flat-topped cuestas of Fluor Island's south side and watching the flash of the Lamb Island lighthouse to the east.

Six-sided "columnar" basalt is formed when a thick lava flow cools and fractures in a honey-comb pattern. The formation on the southwest side of Simpson Island is similar to that of the famed Giant's Causeway in Ireland.

The next day we hopscotched our way between outer islands, paddling by compass bearing in the fog across open water and tracing the narrow, intimate, river-like channels of teal-green water between sphagnum-draped Borden and Spain islands. On the latter, we found a sauna called "Bahia Espana" and painted camouflage to blend in with the brushy shore. But we bypassed it in favour of seeking out the sauna and cabin at Whiskey Cove on Swede Island. We pretty near circumnavigated the island before beaching our kayaks in a shallow bay and stumbling upon a rustic, tar- and cotton-chinked log steam bath with a cylinder-shaped stove, cracked window, rickety door and slivery bench, and a smallish wood-panelled bunkhouse. We were incredulous at what we'd found. Amidst the damp fog and cool air of spring, we'd discovered a private paradise where we would enjoy our second sauna in four days, and trade our damp tent for the warm, dry confines of the quaint cabin.

We need not have been so surprised. There are more people of Finnish descent living around the northwestern reaches of Lake Superior than anywhere outside of Finland, the self-proclaimed "nation of the sauna." The moniker is well-earned: In Finland, there is one sauna for every three people. And as Finns immigrated to northwestern Ontario largely to work in the forest industry, so did their national bath. Community bathhouses like Thunder Bay's Kangas Sauna still draw standing-room-only crowds most every day of the week.

The tradition transcends cultural backgrounds with Scandinavians and Canadians of other descents enjoying the custom. Thunder Bay native and pleasure boater Roger Bailey resurrected the sauna and small cabin at Swede Island from an old mining camp. All along the north shore islands from the Minnesota border at Pigeon River to the communities of Rossport and Terrace Bay, there are at least half a dozen first-come, first-serve saunas like the ones we found tucked behind the shoreline greenery, serving as meeting places for boaters and important safe havens in case of emergency.

For traditionalists, the process of having a sauna isn't hasty. For starters, pronounce it "sow-na," not "saw-na," as it has been corrupted by North Americans. Gather the driest wood you can find and heat the steam bath slowly. Then cut leafy whisks from the tips of birch tree branches that are used in the sauna to slap one's body to increase blood circulation to the skin. These are best harvested in the spring when the leaves cling more tenaciously to the branches and fill the sauna with a pungent, vinegary aroma that's almost intoxicating.

Once the sauna is hot — the Finnish Sauna Society recommends sixty to eighty degrees centigrade — strip down and get in. Don't be sheepish — your birthday suit is always best. Alternate hot sessions in the sauna with cold splashes of air and water. Don't forget *loyly*. Afterwards, you should feel thoroughly rejuvenated — pleasantly subdued, cleaner than you've ever felt before, and, if you suffer from an addictive personality like Dave and me, you might be hooked on the spirit of the sauna forever.

Ahead of schedule after our marathon second day, we spent two days at Swede Island, hiking its perimeter in search of agates and flotsam treasures, cutting and splitting a new supply of firewood, and soaking in the sauna another three times. Were it not for our limited food supplies (by then the hot dogs had been played out) I'm not sure if we would've ever left, playing a Scandinavian version of Robinson Crusoe on a desert island in Lake Superior.

On our last night, we gazed across the eight-kilometre-wide gulf of Black Bay toward the Sleeping Giant. The crossing between our campsite on Porphyry Island and the Sibley Peninsula is the longest stretch of open water en route, a challenge we'd face the next morning. The scene was intimidating: fog swirled over the water's surface and blended into a crimson sky, just above the distinctive, massive form of the Sleeping Giant.

Dave and I had grown accustomed to the amenities of Swede Island and when we left, we wondered where else we might've found other hidden saunas. No doubt there were more — at the abandoned fish camp on Bowman Island and the active one on Magnet Island, and lurking forgotten behind the few ramshackle cabins we saw scattered along the way. The native Ojibwa people

Dave Patterson navigates the seven-hundred-island archipelago of northwestern Lake Superior, in search of a sauna before the storm.

did their own kind of sauna at Wilson Island's Sweat Lodge Point, a sweeping cobblestone beach with a sunset view clear to the horizon.

We longed for the smell of hot cedar, the steamy head rush of *loyly*, and, to a lesser extent, the painful but euphoric feeling of launching one's hot, sweaty self into near-freezing water. For a minute, we mused that the mist swirling in the distance was *loyly* radiating from the biggest steam bath in the world. But, returning to our senses, we remembered it was only fog rising from the largest, coldest freshwater lake in the world. With only two days left on this trip, we would have no more saunas. Darkness fell, and we dragged our feet to the tent.

CHAPTER 9

Mountains Out of Molehills

On the morning of our wedding day, Kim, my wife-to-be, our best friends, and I backcountry skied in the hardwood hills just north of Sault Ste. Marie. In our usual fashion, we planned our wedding ceremony around outdoor adventure. Initially we worried that our December solstice wedding day would be too early in the season for backcountry skiing, but in 2008, the Lake Superior snowmaker rewarded us with ample white stuff to play in. Fittingly, our morning-only ski session extended well into the afternoon, leaving us fashionably late for lunch and rushed to dress and prepare for the late-afternoon ceremony.

Our friend Enn Poldmaa had something to do with Kim and me nearly missing our wedding. Enn is an inveterate telemark skier and the owner of Bellevue Valley Lodge, a small bed and breakfast located in the Algoma Highlands in the community of Goulais River. It's been over a decade since I met Enn and his partner, Robin MacIntyre, on a canoe trip in the then newly formed Algoma Headwaters Provincial Park. I was taken by the couple's concern for the environment, no-frills hippie ethics, love for Canadian folk music, and intrigued by their passion for the obscure sport of telemark skiing, a hybrid Nordic/alpine discipline with Scandinavian roots that's practised by a relative few, generally in the skiing meccas of western Canada. That winter, Enn and Robin invited me to the network of backcountry trails they've carved out of the hilly forest that fringes their rural property.

Even after ten years of telemark skiing, I still feel like a novice. Maybe it's because I don't have Enn's fearlessness or Robin's fine-tuned sense of balance, or perhaps because my telemarking is always tempered by a greater passion for cross-country skiing on the vast networks of groomed trails that surround my home in Sault Ste. Marie. But there's nothing like a sunny, blue-sky day of backcountry skiing with friends when the snow is deep, soft, untracked, and urging you to take one more run — just like my wedding day.

• • •

On a silvery February morning, Enn Poldmaa shuffles impatiently and seems oblivious to the motley eccentricities of the twenty-odd backcountry skiers who have assembled at his bed-and-breakfast home in the small community of Goulais River, just north of Sault Ste. Marie. Local Jorma Paloniemi makes last-minute adjustments to his homemade helmet cam — a waterproof digital point-and-shoot camera that's attached to a yellow whitewater kayak helmet with a piece of bent aluminum canoe gunwale. Enn's brother Alar, who also lives in Goulais, and is dressed in a camouflage fleece jacket and yellow ski pants with red duct tape knee patches, hastily crayons sticky Swix Violet Special to the bases of his telemark skis, apparently vying for the title of world's largest grip-wax pocket. A dozen or so other skiers, including the third Poldmaa brother, Tarmo, who made the two-hour trip down the Trans-Canada from the town of Wawa, are stepping into gear that varies from vintage Karhu skis with old-school rat-trap bindings and neon early-nineties Rossignols, to the latest rocker-tipped, water-ski-shaped powder boards and powerful bindings. Meanwhile, amicable American Mark Stoppel chatters non-stop about his excitement to ski the foot of fresh powder that blankets the Algoma Highlands.

"Ready to go?" barks Enn.

"Rollin'," Paloniemi replies. Before anyone else can respond, the scraggly bearded, wild-haired Estonian-Canadian takes off like a fat-skied Jackrabbit Johannsen, charging toward the five hundred hectares of chutes and glades that make up his backyard. The filmmaker Finn follows in hot pursuit, leaving the rest of us kicking and gliding behind. So begins Ontario's only backcountry ski festival.

Enn Poldmaa and his partner, Robin MacIntyre, have hosted the Snowflea Telefest at their Bellevue Valley Lodge in Goulais River, Ontario, since 1996. They named the festival after the tiny black "springtail" insects that dot the snow on mild, late-winter days. "We thought the name was fitting because snowfleas are just like backcountry skiers," says MacIntyre. "They're gregarious and they hop around in the snow. They're also the first harbinger of spring."

Up to fifty skiers come to the event from across Ontario and the U.S. midwestern states to ski the seven-hundred-odd vertical feet of diverse terrain where the Poldmaa clan and brothers Mark, Joel, and Chris Stoppel, from Traverse

City, Michigan, have carved nearly twenty backcountry runs. For telemark skiers in these parts, Telefest weekend is the highlight of the ski season, which begins with a brush-clearing weekend in November and in good years extends well into the slushy days of May. The hardwood-cloaked Algoma Highlands are just downwind of Lake Superior, which generates consistent lake-effect snow squalls amounting to well over three metres of annual accumulation. Referring to one legendary winter in the nineties, Enn says, "We had sixty straight days of powder skiing, all in dry snow."

A chance meeting of the Stoppels and Poldmaas in the mid-1980s heralded the beginning of telemark skiing in the "bush" of northern Ontario. The Stoppels were regulars at Sault Ste. Marie's Searchmont Resort, and inquired about Enn's upstart bed-and-breakfast operations. On their first visit, the telemarking Stoppels "discovered" the virgin descents of Enn's back forty, and decided that earning powder turns was better than lapping Searchmont's groomed runs. "I remember the first time we skied back there," says Mark Stoppel. "I told Enn, 'you've got *real* ski hills back there, man.' We did some exploring, discovered endless terrain, and realized we could ski here for the rest of our lives."

Being veteran cross-country and alpine skiers, MacIntyre and the brothers Poldmaa were quick to pick up telemark skiing. Although the sport's origins are as simple as downhill skiing on cross-country gear, telemark equipment has evolved to become similar to alpine. Modern telemark ski boots are plastic and supportive, and backcountry skis are metal-edged and typically wide like alpine skis to offer better floatation in soft snow.

"For a couple of years we were jumping around on 215-centimetre-long, double-camber wooden cross-country skis," says Enn. "The Stoppels had adapted downhill skis to telemark bindings. They were the first people I met using wider, shorter skis for backcountry skiing."

About the only part of telemark skiing that bears any resemblance to its centuries-old Norwegian roots are the "freeheel" bindings, which allow the foot to flex in each turn. This also enables more comfortable touring with the use of grip waxes and skins — removable, grippy strips of fabric that are used for ascending steeper slopes.

Even though the activity is considered a "fringe" sport in much of Canada, Algoma's long-standing Scandinavian heritage has made it a stronghold of skiers who prefer exploring the untracked woods to following groomed trails

Enn Poldmaa and Cedar Snowbounder make tracks in the hardwood-cloaked hills of Goulais River. Each year, winter begins with a trail-clearing day where Poldmaa secures a government permit and rustles up a crew of backcountry ski enthusiasts to lop saplings and brush, opening up runs for downhill skiing.

or riding chairlifts. "Backcountry skiing is more of a do-it-yourself thing," says Stoppel. "It's something you get addicted to. It's been two or three years since I last rode a chairlift at a ski resort."

On the hill, the Poldmaas' hard-driving, war-whooping, don't-mess-with-my-line style somehow meshes with the Stoppels' more laid-back approach to create a powerful, if unlikely, bloodline-transcending synergy. "There's a strange parallel," says Enn. "They're three brothers and we're three brothers. Some of the best ski runs of my life have involved the six of us skiing together, flying and zigzagging through the trees and just nailing our lines." Mark remembers the brothers' first run on a newly cut line in the deepest snow he's ever skied. "Sometimes you have to be cautious with Enn's snow reports," he says. "But that day, man, I tell ya, the snow was going over Enn's shoulders. We literally couldn't speak when the six of us came out at the bottom … we were all just euphoric."

After a couple of strides, my gluey skis become less grabby and soon I'm tight on Enn's heels as we tour from the lodge into the adjacent public Crown land that comprises a portion of the rugged Algoma Highlands, which stretches like a halo of wilderness around Lake Superior northwest of Sault Ste. Marie. Like the Poldmaa brothers, I've plastered my skis with a layer of sticky wax for traction on the climb. Each year more and more Telefest skiers seem to become corrupted by climbing skins, essentially a carpet-like material that attaches to the skis' bases with a peel-and-stick, reusable adhesive, but the event's Nordic purists abhor the hassle of continually needing to attach and remove skins while "yo-yoing" short runs. "People do fine with the skins, but you always hear them saying, 'hey, you're getting in more runs than I am,'" says Enn. It's a fact that grip wax is far faster on the flats, and with a bit of technique and a few more switchbacks, the Poldmaas go out of their way to prove that it's more than capable on the climb.

The ascent from Bellevue Valley Lodge traverses an undulating cedar swamp before emerging through a veil of spruce and trending decidedly uphill through a mature maple forest. This slope is known as "Tele One" — the most beginner-friendly run in the area. But even the so-called green run is challenging, largely because of the significant number of two- to three-foot diameter maples that litter the hill like immovable slalom gates. It's an especially intimidating sight for a beginner, and I remember my first time here, grunting my way uphill, secretly hoping the climb would never end to avoid the certain perils of bombing the descent. The best piece of advice that Enn ever gave me was to watch out for the less common yellow and white birch trees, which blend into the snow and have a tendency to sneak up on you when you least expect it.

Once we reach the top of the forty-degree, tree-covered slope, another skier, Monika Jost, stomps the snow off her skis and whispers, "I kinda got the chickens right now." Moments after Jost divulges her apprehension, Enn goes flying by, dropping a knee with each turn, carving graceful arcs in the metre-deep snow and leaving spindrift in his wake. It's just the inspiration Jost needs. The high school principal, former provincial downhill ski racer, and outdoor enthusiast from Sudbury takes a deep breath and points her skis down the hill, making her first turns in the powdery snow.

Now it's my turn. I mimic Enn's trademark shuffle-step to remove the mass of snow that clings to the bases of skis and make my first descent of the day, floating through dry, knee-deep powder. Surprisingly, the gooey grip wax is barely discernable as I glide downhill through the maples. When I meet up with her at bottom of the run, Jost takes a brief moment to catch her breath and admire the arcing S-turns we've made in the snow. "Let's do it again!" she enthuses. The hoots and hollers of the rest of the crew can be heard through the trees as we stomp our grippy skis back uphill.

Telefest became somewhat less entertaining when my friend Jorma Paloniemi replaced his hot-pink and sky-blue ski jacket, cheap, department-store ski pants, and an ancient army surplus backpack. A new permanent job as an aerial photo interpreter with the provincial government's Ministry of Natural Resources means the forty-nine-year-old can now afford the latest high-tech waterproof-breathable shells and snow-pant bibs. "Oh, I still miss that jacket," says the quirky, unassuming, first-generation Finnish-Canadian. "I've never really believed in Gore-Tex and that was the most photogenic jacket I ever had."

About the same time as his reluctant makeover, Paloniemi's second knee-rebuild limited his once hard-charging style. Paloniemi mentored my progress as a telemark skier in between launching ten-metre cliffs on

Batchawana Mountain, a remote, snow-machine-access peak with over one thousand feet of prime snowbelt elevation one hundred kilometres north of Sault Ste. Marie. Back then, Paloniemi ripped it on old-school, narrow-waisted skis, a brace supporting the knee he initially blew out while ski-patrolling and living out of the back of a pick-up truck in the legendary British Columbia resort town of Fernie in the early nineties. "I won't do the cliff jumps anymore," is his stock reply to my urges to let loose.

But in the perfect "hero" snow conditions we have today, Paloniemi still skis harder than most. Late in the morning, I catch him scoping and skiing a steep and challenging line down a cascade of granite pillows. He skis like a zephyr, arms spread out for balance, and body flowing from turn to turn in a graceful poetry of motion. When we tour further afield for an afternoon session on the Poldmaas' and Stoppels' beloved North Face runs, which boast as much elevation and advanced terrain as any ski resort in Ontario, a dozen of us stop to watch as Paloniemi matches Enn in an impromptu, high-speed game of turn for turn, his eyes focused intensely on the viewfinder of his helmet cam. Catcalls and cheers erupt when Enn catches an edge, face-plants in the powder and is barely sidestepped by Paloniemi, who finishes the run clean. "Wow, eh," he says, wheezing for air. "Gonna have to replay that one."

The "North Face" features advanced backcountry terrain with steep chutes and cliffs. Here Jorma Paloniemi finishes a run on Season's Pass with his trademark helmet-cam rolling.

Besides operating a bed and breakfast and a landscaping business, Enn Poldmaa and Robin MacIntyre are ardent promoters of Canadian folk music, hence the names of some of their favourite ski runs.

The gentler southerly facing slopes we skied in the morning are nothing compared to the longer, steeper, tree-covered glades of the North Face. There's enough variety and brushed-out terrain here that we mine fresh powder until sunset, never skiing a run more than once. The Northwest Passage leads to Shaky Jake, named after Enn's favourite ski dog. Next in line is Big Music, then the Vortex, which funnels off a steep pitch through a stand of ancient cedars, and finally Season's Pass. The aptly named latter is comprised of at least three quad-burning runs. After each descent we're lucky enough to stomp our way back to the top on the same well-packed uptrail, which takes about forty minutes to ascend. On one descent, Alar leads the charge along a narrow ridge that appears to end in a cliff. "Just trust it," he says, slowing momentarily before launching his camouflage-clad body over the precipice. Beyond my better judgment, I follow him to the lip. Four desperate turns later and I, too, am at the base of the triangular-shaped, fifty-degree Pyramid of Denial, the area's newest run.

In a good afternoon, the most dedicated Telefest skiers will climb and descend nearly 4,500 vertical feet — not bad for mid-continent backcountry. Late in the afternoon, my wife, Kim, Michigan-based enthusiast Mike Everetts, and I make our last run and slowly make our way back to the lodge in the waning light of February twilight. It's all we can do to make the climb up the aptly named Undertaker and ski the friendly — if heavily tracked and pockmarked by the imprints of fallen skiers — slopes of Tele One back to the lodge.

According to Scandinavian tradition, the session ends with a sauna, where half a dozen or so naked and exhausted men (the women have their turn, too) crowd the benches and soak up the heat, occasionally running outside to drop through the ice into Enn's fish pond. Paloniemi and I indulge in our own Telefest ritual in the sauna, passing a sickeningly warm bottle of Olde English malt liquor back and forth, chalking it up as good luck that no one else will accept our "horse piss" drink. "It's the malt liquor, really," muses Paloniemi, showing the signs of the combined effect of heat, dehydration, and a bit of alcohol. "That's what I'm here for." All too soon the bottle runs dry and we stumble through the snow to take our last dunking. But over at the lodge, the party — and planning for tomorrow — is just getting started.

CHAPTER 10

The Beachcombers

Once upon a time, Lake Superior's north shore was a busy place. Before sea lamprey depleted commercial fish stocks, fishermen set nets for lake trout, whitefish, and herring on the shoals and lived in bustling outports like the village at Gargantua in present-day Lake Superior Provincial Park, and Quebec Harbour on Michipicoten Island. Before feller-bunchers eliminated the need for axemen, skidders replaced horses, and tractor trailers outdated tugboats and log booms, lumbermen drove millions of cords of pulpwood down Lake Superior's tributary rivers and powerful tugs hauled the logs offshore to distant mills. About the same time, trappers ranged the coastline and interior throughout the winter months, creating a web of trails and cabins and a staunch yet little-known, hardscrabble, yet often sociable, bush community.

Fewer in number were the beachcombers — the men and women who worked like ants along the lakeshore, rounding up the thousands of logs that escaped the two-kilometre-long booms on their way to the mill. Heron Bay's McCuaig family derived much of their income this way for more than three decades starting in the mid-1930s. They also dabbled in ushering recreational fishermen and prospectors, government workers and outdoor enthusiasts up and down the coast as the logging industry dried up. Today, Marathon resident Keith McCuaig is the last in the line of beachcombers. Though he no longer rustles up logs from remote beaches, he still ekes out some semblance of a living on the lake through his charter service, keeping the family tradition alive.

I only met Keith's father, Bruce, in passing, but by all accounts he was a character. Bruce was famous for his stories and sense of humour, as well as his chronic affinity for drinking can after can of Pepsi; at times, the deck of his cherished blue, thirty-eight-foot welded steel tug, the Century, resembled a recycling depot. The coast isn't nearly as busy as it was in his father's and especially his grandfather's day, but Keith McCuaig is a living link to the past. I've spent some memorable hours with the man whose swagger on land suggests a greater comfort at sea and whose humble tales reflect a life spent on Lake Superior.

. . .

Keith McCuaig still remembers when the rivers flowing into Lake Superior flowed thick with eight-foot logs of balsam fir and spruce destined for the pulp and paper mills that once dotted the lake's periphery from Sault Ste. Marie to Thunder Bay. Pulp logs were cut in the winter and piled alongside rivers to await the spring freshet. When the icy rivers broke up, adrenaline-charged loggers would use pick-poles and dynamite to break up jams, ushering the logs to the lake. There the logs were picked up by tugs, boomed into massive rafts measuring the size of multiple football fields, and towed at a snail's pace to the nearest mill, often hundreds of kilometres away.

Inevitably, booms broke up in rough weather and countless pulp logs washed up on the beaches of the north shore. That's where Keith comes in, a third-generation beachcomber who was ultimately run out of the trade by the end of the river-drive era, but who still embodies the old happy-go-lucky lifestyle, scraping a living plying the big water of Lake Superior. "It was a simplish concept, really," says Keith in his characteristically impish, unassuming way. "We were the salvage guys." I've joined him for a day on *Melissa June*, the thirty-foot twin-hull aluminum powerboat he uses to jockey sea kayakers, canoeists,

Keith McCuaig at the helm of the Melissa June, *the thirty-foot catamaran-style shore-landing boat he purchased in 2008.*

and hikers up and down the Lake Superior coast from his home port of Heron Bay, just south of Marathon, to catch a glimpse of a day in his life and to hear stories about his life on the lake.

On this foggy mid-July morning, Keith settles into storytelling as we leisurely motor back to port after dropping off seven sea kayakers at the remote east end of Michipicoten Island. McCuaig's family ties are firmly anchored in Lake Superior. His great-grandfather from his mother's side, David Coveney, kept the Hawkins Island lighthouse at the entrance to Peninsula Harbour, near present-day Marathon, from 1920 to 1945. Coveney has a street named after him overlooking the lake in Marathon.

His paternal side, meanwhile, came to Heron Bay via Port Arthur (Thunder Bay) in the 1930s. Keith's grandfather, Kenneth Thompson (nicknamed KT, after whom Keith is named), got his start in the pulp salvage business almost immediately. KT piloted the venerable *Bern M.*, a diesel-powered tug named after his wife. His territory covered hundreds of kilometres of coastline, virtually from Michipicoten Bay in the east and stretching north to the old railway town of Jackfish, near present-day Terrace Bay. Working the inshore waters, KT would've known the coastline intimately.

"Our job was to pick up the stuff that got away and sell it back to the mills," says Keith, scanning the milky horizon through his thick eyeglasses. "We'd round up the logs on the beaches with pickeroons [metal-spiked poles used to manoeuvre logs] and tow them by boat to Marathon. Sometimes the beaches would be piled high with logs."

Beachcombing was seasonal work comprising only a part of KT's year. Keith tells me that his grandfather also trapped, spending long, cold winters in the bush in isolated places like the Pukaskwa River and Mud Bay (now Hattie Cove, the headquarters of Pukaskwa National Park). Once he overwintered with bushman Gus Weideman, a notorious character with mysterious origins who arrived on the northeastern shore of Lake Superior via Europe in 1924 and immediately became a legend. Weideman was an enigma — feared by game wardens, respected by peers, reputedly able to lift four-hundred-pound barrels of coal oil single-handedly, said to bet boaters he could ride on a moose's back (and once breaking his leg in the process), and a well-spoken, intelligent man who kept up to date on world events. He was said to have drilled shotgun-barrel-sized holes in the door of his Otter Cove trap cabin to scare away snooping wardens.

Keith's father, Bruce, picked up the beachcombing gig and built on KT's interest in shuttling sport fishermen and tourists up and down the roadless coast as a sideline. Instead of trapping, he spent his winters running the general store and hotel in the community of Heron Bay. As logging patterns changed and concentrated on the White River, a major waterway located twenty-five kilometres south of Marathon, the McCuaigs' territory narrowed to the surrounding area. They'd typically range south as far as Triangle Harbour, in the heart of today's Pukaskwa National Park, and north to the Coldwell Peninsula.

Keith remembers spending many a day as a youngster, wind-, wave-, or fogbound along the coast. "We always seemed to get stuck north of Marathon — Sturdee Cove, Port Munro, and Detention Island," he says. "Back then we didn't have radar, so Dad wasn't keen to go out in the fog. It meant we spent a lot of days stuck in one place, especially in the spring." On these days, Bruce used to say, "The lake is going to do what it's going to do. There's no sense in worrying about it."

The Kushick brothers from Michipicoten Harbour trapped along the Pukaskwa coast in the 1920s and 1930s, about the time KT McCuaig was getting started as a pulp log salvager. Frank Kushick carved his name in several shoreline rocks between Marathon and Michipicoten, including this one near the mouth of the Pipe River.

Eventually, his father's cherished *Bern M.* was sold and Bruce went looking for another boat to cruise the coast. He found the *Century*, a partially enclosed, trawler-style tug built in 1974 in the Lake Erie community of Port Stanley, Ontario, to celebrate the town's centennial. Bruce quickly fell in love with the *Century*. "He really thought it was the perfect boat," recalls Keith. "It had a reputation of being good in a sea and because the engine was in the bow there was lots of space in her." For his part, Bruce is remembered for calling the hard-working and reliable *Century* "the best boat on the Great Lakes."

With the new boat, Keith and his brother, Neil, convinced their old man to get up to speed on modern navigational technology. "We bugged Dad for years to get such a thing as radar," says Keith. "When he finally gave in and got one installed he said, 'Holy crap, now I can see where I'm going in the fog!'"

With the creation of Pukaskwa National Park in 1983 came a new wave of adventure tourists to replace the trappers, fishermen, and loggers who once populated the coast. The *Century* gave Bruce the means to usher backpackers into Pukaskwa's roadless interior and move sea kayakers and canoeists up and down the coast. With outdoor recreation and sea-kayaking in particular spiking in popularity in the 1990s, the McCuaigs caught a glimpse of their future working on the lake.

I'd wager that Keith McCuaig, like his father and grandfather, could describe every mile of coastline between his home port of Heron Bay south to the Pukaskwa River. He's travelled this section of Lake Superior every summer of his life in a small navy of boats, small and large. Most of the bays come with stories. There's Pulpwood Harbour, a narrow, spruce-lined fjord where his father and grandfather used to store booms of logs en route to the mill. The McCuaigs used to keep cabins at Picture Rock Harbour, an island-dotted, horseshoe-shaped bay just north of the White River, and Simons Harbour, a scenic cove sheltered by a screen of islands and rimmed by rounded one-hundred-metre-tall hills that flow inland like waves on the lake.

If the coves and bays mean safety, the countless rock headlands jutting into Lake Superior represent the lake's fickle demeanor. "When you go around Ogilvie Point, Sewell Point, and Otter Head, you know something's going to happen," says Keith. Over the years he's observed different weather patterns on the lake. For instance, if he's heading north and conditions are "dirty" and rough south of Sewell Point, a flattened slab of rock knifing into Superior near Pukaskwa National Park's Oiseau Bay, he'll usually push on because sea conditions will likely moderate north of the point. "You learn to read the weather and how things change along the coast," says Keith. "But you never *really* know what it's going to do. So mostly you go by gut feeling. Sometimes I do okay."

Keith likes to tell the story about when he was courting Melissa Yee, a woman he met while going to Wilfred Laurier University and who later moved north with him and became his wife. "We did a run down the coast in a little metal punt with a 9.9 horsepower engine," he says. "The wind and waves came up and we ducked into Trapper's Harbour," a small, rocky inlet located about eighty kilometres south of Heron Bay. "The shoals make it a tricky place to get out of when the weather's dirty and we were stuck there for two and a half days. Luckily I never travel light and Melissa and I did okay."

As the storm slowly abated and their provisions ran low, Keith and his wife-to-be beelined for home in "fog, rain," and generally "dirty" sea conditions. Travelling point to point that afternoon, he recalls meeting up with his father, who was shuttling a group of paddlers down the coast. "Dad was telling his customers, 'Now who the hell is this idiot way out on the big lake in such a small boat?'" Keith says. "But I don't think he was really surprised when I hailed him on the radio and said it was me."

As a teenager, Keith saw few opportunities in northern Ontario. The quality of his education deteriorated the further he went in public school and, at the age of sixteen, he chose to move to Toronto to live with his brother, Neil, to finish high school. He admits that "I thought I'd never move back" when he enrolled at Wilfred Laurier University in Waterloo and graduated with a degree in business administration.

Then came a chance opportunity in 1994 to move back to Marathon and work as a controller for Pic River First Nation. It was a great stroke of luck when Melissa, who grew up in southern Ontario, was game to pack up and move north, where she's since taken a job working in human resources for the town of Marathon. Keith has never regretted coming home. "I could never live down there again," he says. "Sometimes we go back to visit. It's crazy. All we want to do is come back home again."

Keith has never been far from the water. When his father passed away in 2002, Keith and Neil took over the family charter service. They purchased *Eagle 22*, a twenty-four-foot aluminum boat with a small cabin that moved

The Melissa June *is capable of carrying up to eight sea kayaks on its cabin top racks. It cruises at around fifty-five kilometres per hour.*

passengers up and down the coast far faster than his father's *Century*. The west coast–style, deep-V boat was fast and sleek — in fact almost too sleek — for the McCuaigs' use. What took a full day in the plodding *Century* could be done in a mere few hours. With the Canadian government angling toward strict regulations in marine charter services, Keith thought that the time was right to invest in a new, bigger boat with more capacity kayaks and greater comfort for passengers, and, unlike other operators, to follow the laws to the letter.

A few years later, he custom-ordered a thirty-foot catamaran-style boat from Port Angeles, Washington. The *Melissa June* features a hydraulically operated drop-down bow to allow passengers easy access to shore — a key feature for shuttling hikers and paddlers to remote drop-off points. It's powered by twin 250-horsepower Yamahas; though these high-tech, computer-operated behemoths don't share the same reassuring guttural groan and powerful torque of the beloved old diesels Keith grew up with, he concedes they're easier to maintain in the long run. Plus they allow the *Melissa June* to skim along the water at fifty-five kilometres per hour compared to the *Century*'s tortoise-like twelve.

As someone most accustomed to travelling in small, paddle-powered boats, I'm always taken aback at how powerboats shrink distance. An effortless, hour-long cruise gets you to a destination that would've involved a gruelling two-day paddle following the contours of the shore. It seems like we've barely loaded up the kayaks and kayakers and left the harbour to shuttle to Michipicoten Island and then we're there, out of the fog and snugged up to the concrete pier at the stalwart East End Lighthouse. After the kayaks are unloaded, we take a few moments to gaze in the windows of the lighthouse keepers' residence and enjoy the silence of one of the most remote places on Lake Superior. "I remember coming out here with Dad when the last lightkeepers still lived here," says Keith.

But as much as our choices in modes of transportation differ, Keith and I are no different in our reasons for cherishing every moment spent on Lake Superior. I ask him to pinpoint his love for the place. "It's the freedom," he tells me without hesitation. "It's being able to go out and not see a person, to explore places I've known all my life" and, most often, to see that they haven't changed. On our return trip, Keith almost seems surprised when another boat shows up on the radar — the only sign of life we've seen in covering over one hundred kilometres of water this morning. "I think it's a sailing vessel," he says, pointing at a dense green blob on the radar screen. "You don't see boats that often out here." Indeed, Lake Superior is a far lonelier place than it was when KT McCuaig plied it in the old *Bern M.*

In fact, it's almost too lonely. Keith's vessel is spotlessly clean, comfortably appointed with an enclosed cabin, "100 percent legal" under the auspices of Transport Canada's Canada Shipping Act, and equipped with thousands of dollars of safety gear, Global Position System navigation, radar and depth sounder technology, and electronics. He's the only operator on the Canadian shore of the lake to have attained these standards, yet there's still barely enough business to make it all worthwhile. In 2010, when Pukaskwa National Park's coastal hiking trail was closed for repairs for the second season in a row, he spent barely a dozen days working on the lake, culminating a decade of inconsistent business.

He's had moderate success adding Lake Superior–based scientific researchers and government workers to his client list, but he's still not on the water as much as he'd like. He tries not to rant about Transport Canada's inability to enforce, administer, and therefore support operators like him who maintain government standards. Still, he's had to take other jobs — working as an administrator for Parks Canada out of Thunder Bay and managing Marathon's hardware store. But he always comes back to the lake; it's in his blood, bred in the bone. "It's just something that I enjoy," he says. "I mean, there's no money in it. No money at all. But perhaps someday if the stars line up my theories will be proven correct."

CHAPTER 11

Guiding Light

I was merely eighteen years old when I started guiding commercial canoe and sea-kayak trips in the Lake Superior basin. Whereas many youngsters get their start leading their teenaged peers at summer camp, I began with adults — usually well-off professionals at least twice my age expecting a fully catered wilderness vacation. The learning curve was steep. I was lucky to be mentored in outdoor cuisine, communication, decision-making, nature interpretation, and paddling skills by the pioneers of the outdoor adventure trade in the Great Lakes area.

As much as many of the vignettes that follow suggest a sense of frustration with guiding sea-kayak and canoe trips, that is certainly not the case. I've met my best friends working for outfitters based in Sault Ste. Marie, Goulais River, and Wawa, as well as the woman who became my wife. I have kept in close contact with many of the clients I have led over the years. There's a great feeling of satisfaction to receive heartfelt words of thanks at the end of a trip, to know that an outdoor experience was deeply resonant. This, I believe, is a huge contribution to developing a community of people willing to stand up for wilderness conservation.

And then there are the simple joys of spending days on end travelling the coastline of Lake Superior. In many ways, guiding forces me to slow down and see the shoreline through the eyes of a diverse range of clientele. There are also fringe benefits. Many times I've decided to stop for the day early and escaped the stress of guiding by striking off for an hour on my own. I'll scramble over the rocks and find a secluded place on glacier-smoothed pink granite and lie in the sun. I'll strip down and slide into the big lake's refreshing green water when I get too hot. At times like this I wonder how the rest of the world gets by, and count myself among the lucky.

The apocalyptic consequences of a capsized tandem sea kayak was one of the first things I learned when I started guiding commercial adventure tours on the Great Lakes over a decade ago. A swamped tandem was too heavy to rescue, said my mentors. No one ever spoke of what to do if one went over. Over the years I've had the "ass clenchers" of guide-speak — when fully loaded, twenty-two-foot fiberglass torpedoes careened through the surf zone or wallowed precariously in an eight-foot swell — but only once has one turtled.

Lake Superior's Pukaskwa coast stretches for 180 roadless kilometres between the northern Ontario hinterland towns of Marathon and Wawa, protected nearly in its entirety by national and provincial parks. The coastline has a personality as split as the lake's notoriously fickle temperament: sheltered sand beaches alternate with towering 150-metre-tall headlands where safe landings are all but impossible. It's a magical shore that's steeped in the Aboriginal myth of Mishepeshu, a giant, restless underwater cat that lashes the lake's ice-cold water into a frenzy.

On a sunny late-May morning, I pulled into the parking lot of the Pukaskwa National Park visitor centre and met my group for a three-day out-and-back run down the coast. My guests were two Ojibwa women who had spent much of their lives along the forested fringe of Lake Superior, but have never seen its coastline from a kayak. We loaded their tandem sea kayak and my single, and I provided a crash course on the wet exit — how to eject from the kayak in case of a capsize — and basic paddle strokes. Then we threaded a rocky gauntlet to the big lake.

A steady breeze and choppy waves had formed by lunch. My guests were comfortable with paddling in the half-metre waves, so after a quick break we pushed another three kilometres to the White River. We made it to the river's mouth with no problems. I scouted the current first, crossing a heaving differential where Lake Superior met a five-kilometre-per-hour current of peaty brown river water that flowed like a tidal stream. There's no way my guests would make it upriver on their own, but I figured I could give them a boost with a towline.

I reinforced the importance of leaning downstream to offset the torque of the roiling intersection of lake and river — known in river-speak as the "eddyline." Then I clipped in with my towline, gathered speed, and crossed into the main stream of the river. Moments later, I felt a gut-wrenching tug and looked back and saw the gleaming white hull of a leviathan kayak that, when fully loaded, weighed at least two hundred pounds.

The author steals away for some time alone and a self-portrait while windbound at Otter Island on a guided sea-kayak trip on the coastline of the Pukaskwa National Park.

This can't be happening, I thought. I released my towbelt to avoid the risk of being keelhauled by the runaway kayak, spun around, and rushed back to the swimmers, both of whom quickly exited the boat and were now fully immersed in the chilly water, floating in life jackets. I started barking out orders — "Hold on to your boat!" — as we drifted into three-foot standing waves that formed at the river mouth. Charged with adrenaline, I somehow manage to right the swamped kayak and pluck the swimmers out of the churning water back into their flooded cockpits. Rafted together and bouncing helplessly in the waves, I tried to formulate a plan while whispering sweet nothings to my panicked guests: "It's okay, take deep breaths, the worst is over." A few moments passed where I honestly didn't know what to do next.

Clarity came when I noticed a Ziploc bag of tobacco floating inside one of the flooded cockpits. To the Ojibwa, tobacco is a powerful medicine that's offered as a sign of respect and, sometimes, a request for fortitude in the face of danger. I scanned the shoreline, spotted a level rock shelf amidst a wall of unfriendly granite, and began manoeuvring our ponderous raft toward it with extended paddle strokes. When we reached shore, I bailed out of my kayak just offshore and again summoned unknown strength to manhandle the kayaks onto the rocks. My guests were shaken, bruised, and cold from being immersed in the ten-degree-Celsius water. We pulled out dry clothes and sleeping bags and within thirty minutes of radioing the national park warden, rescue teams in an inflatable Zodiac powerboat and a big Boston Whaler abruptly ended our trip.

I'd come a long way to be left to my own devices in dealing with an over-turned kayak in icy-cold water along a rugged coastline. I came to outdoor adventure leadership as a teenaged volunteer, joining a five-day canoe trip on the Sand River in Lake Superior Provincial Park primarily to haul gear on its countless portages and to act as a whitewater safety boat for well-to-do adventure tourists from Canada, the United States, and Great Britain. I never worked so hard in my life, but neither had I seen the thrills and revelations of city people on their first wilderness experience.

Commercial tripping, I quickly realized, was as much about pampering guests with gourmet meals as it was about paddling. I learned how to chop onions and garlic and how to make coffee and oatmeal in the bush. But because of the Sand River's tedious portages and our delayed departures in the mornings, the work was as gruelling as the days were long. On the last night, as we were washing dishes by moonlight, the lead guide and trip coordinator, Tarmo Poldmaa, offered me a job for the season. I excitedly accepted.

That summer I guided three more wilderness canoe trips, including a back-breaking five-day outing in the height of blackfly and mosquito season where my co-guide and I estimated we lugged gear and canoes over thirty-five kilometres of portages. My feet were bloodied and blistered in shredded sandals, my body covered in bug bites. I swore and cursed a lot behind clients' backs, and started to appreciate that guiding is less about a dreamy life of days on end in the wilderness and rather a combination of physical grunt work and the complex challenge of making urbanites comfortable with themselves and each other in decidedly foreign terrain — all for minuscule daily remuneration amounting to a fraction of minimum wage. I started at $60 per day.

Mostly that first summer I learned about what goes on behind the scenes to make trips work: white-knuckling underpowered jalopies down the Trans-Canada Highway en route to a trip starting point, hoping they didn't break down while the paying customers were on board; illegally installing trailer hitches on rental trucks and using them to tow overloaded boat trailers when company vehicles were in short supply; packing food for an extended guided trip the night before departure day in my mother's kitchen; and sitting around a campfire from sunset to sunrise at a friend's cottage, drinking beer and revelling in the indescribable sense of freedom of responsibility when the clients leave and another trip is done.

Despite the stress, responsibility, and poor pay, there is an element of carefree fun in guiding that I think recreates the *joie de vie* experienced by the fur-trading voyageurs of centuries ago. It is liberating to work in an environment that's far removed from micro-managing supervisors, and both frightening and exciting to know that if things go sideways you'll have to be the first to respond. Early on in my career, monsoon rains and gale-force winds interrupted a sea-kayak festival we were hosting at Agawa Bay, sending the clients home in a soggy mass exodus a day early. Later that night, we gathered beneath a partially collapsed circus tent, passed around bottles of liquor and watched as the storm moved offshore, its bolts of lightning hitting the lake and setting the sky on fire. We knew that come morning we'd be making contingency plans to deal with the lousy weather, but at the time we were living in the moment — a key character trait of any outdoor leader.

Guide Scott Roesch prepares dinner on Day One of a guided canoe trip on the Sand River.
Elaborate backcountry meals are part and parcel with the guided trip experience.

I started out a diehard canoeist, adamant that I would only lead canoe trips. When it became obvious that sea-kayaking was a way to spend more time in the wilderness, I reluctantly became a convert — and then, rapidly, an enthusiast. As a university student, I worked from late May to early September, guiding trips up and down the Lake Superior coastline, spending the odd night in roadside motels, hastily re-provisioning for the next trip in places like Wawa, Marathon, or Terrace Bay, then meeting another group and heading out again. I got to know the shoreline well, my maps annotated with scribbled notes as I amassed a lifetime of experience in a few summers of continuous trips. I also got to know many of the clients — schoolteachers, lawyers, doctors, and retired entrepreneurs from places like Detroit, Minneapolis, and Toronto — friends who returned year after year on their summer vacation.

Each expedition was different for its variable weather, the occasional misadventure, and quirky, idiosyncratic clients. One trip blended into the next, and twelve years became a black hole of events. But just like how some stars stand out in the night sky, some memories burn brighter than others.

It's a moment when I should've known better. "Can you make us a campfire? Pleeease?" whined one of my clients. It's sunset on the last night of a four-day sea-kayak trip in Lake Superior Provincial Park in my second year of guiding. My group came to Lake Superior as strangers and will be leaving as friends, largely on account of their proclivity for drinking vast quantities of alcohol. And just when I thought they'd run the stores dry, plans for a big blowout are coming together — all they need is a bonfire.

I kindle a small fire with pieces of driftwood and immediately realize my mistake. As it happened, they still had plenty of booze, plus the bag of wine I'd packed to sip with dinner. Some of the men in the group haul in a couple of monster logs and toss them on the fire. As the clients stumble around the blaze, I realize I'm in for a long night of babysitting, lest someone get burned. The night is a bipolar mix of awkward drunken confessions and tears offset by manic singing and dancing. With only a day's turnaround to pack for my next trip, all I want to do is go to bed; I'm acutely aware that I'll be the first one up in the morning, cooking breakfast, making coffee, and rousing my hungover troops.

The next day, when we finally get around to getting on the water, finish the trip, and load boats on the trailer for the drive back to base, my clients dig into their pockets and slip me wads of bills — tips for cooking, fire-making, and keeping them safe. Meanwhile I'm exhausted, flaked out in the van, and wondering if it's really worth it.

A thick, moody fog hangs over the lake as we load our kayaks into an ancient fishing tug and slowly motor for four long hours to Pukaskwa River, where we'll start a five-day paddling trip north along the coastline of Pukaskwa National Park. I spend the morning snoozing fitfully amidst a pile of gear. After two weeks of continuous tripping, my employer has graciously commissioned an assistant, Linda, to handling the cooking on this trip. She's packed a small mountain of food to address the dietary needs of the vegetarians and carnivores in our five-person group, all packed in bulky plastic boxes that I doubt will ever fit in the hatches of our kayaks. I have no idea what's on the menu, but I'm looking forward to enjoying someone else's cooking for a change.

And then the accident happens. We're loading boats into the water, preparing to launch one hundred metres offshore. Linda slips and a laden kayak crushes her finger against the sharp metal edge of the boat. There is blood, confusion, and cries of pain. Then Linda is on the ground convulsing, her finger broken and dangling by a few shreds of flesh. I struggle to remember my first-aid training: Attack the wound with well-aimed direct pressure. Slowly, Linda regains her wits. She insists we get on with the trip, and I agree to leave her only after I've wrapped her injured digit and talked with the boat captain to ensure he could give her a ride to the hospital in Wawa. We eventually launch our kayaks — now ponderously overloaded with boxes of food — and paddle in silence into the dark, depressing fog.

Somehow things work out. I experiment with Linda's oversupply of foods and the weather turns beautiful after the Day One fog. At trip's end, we're surprised to see Linda waiting for us at the take-out. Her finger has been successfully reattached, and she can't wait to hear about our adventures.

I first noticed that Jerry was different when he insisted we use only "primitive tools" — rocks and sticks — to split up a log of cedar he found on a cobblestone beach for our evening campfire. Most people prefer to relax after a long day of paddling, but not Jerry. While others laze in the sun, make obsessive-compulsive

Milwaukee, Wisconsin, resident Jerry Nowak paddles the Pukaskwa coast in 2010. Nowak has participated in a half-dozen guided sea-kayak and canoe trips along Lake Superior's north shore.

adjustments to their tent and gear, or read, Jerry, a middle-aged social worker from Wisconsin, bushwhacks along the shore in search of swimming holes and jumping cliffs, hikes up rivers, and devises survival challenges and feats of strength for the rest of the group to reluctantly partake in. On this evening, our beach just happens to be laced with smaller, fire-worthy pieces of driftwood, but he insists we all take part in a sort of "Caveman Games" — attempting to split up this big chunk of wood by hand.

Jerry knows Lake Superior as well as anyone. For over twenty years he's made a habit of road-tripping here in his trademark beat-up vehicles. He's a self-proclaimed "freeloader," camping in roadside pull-offs, doing a bit of kayaking or canoeing, berry-picking, and, of course, swimming. He idolizes Canadian canoeing icon Bill Mason and revels in stories about the voyageurs. I call him the "Man of the North" or, as he prefers it, *L'Homme du Nord*. He paddles a short, sluggish kayak that retailers would call a "rec" boat, yet he easily keeps pace with the other long, sleek sea kayaks. The guy is a dynamo, a group-builder, capable paddler, and a true joy to have on a trip.

I wonder if his demeanor at home in Milwaukee is as good as it is on Lake Superior. On one trip, he made sure that his first-time trip-mate rode in the front seat of the van en route to our starting point for the best view of the scenery. On another, he got in the habit of pulling out his gas stove and "kittle" each day at lunch and providing the group with cups of tea. He told us how much he'd love to set up a backwoods coffee shop along the coast and spend the summer greeting (and surprising) paddlers mid-trip. "Chief, do we have time for a boil-up?" he'd ask. Uncertain weather had to wait; for Jerry, I could never refuse.

The bear wanders into camp at sunset. I'm leading Parks Canada employees on a staff reconnaissance sea-kayaking trip along the coastline of Pukaskwa National Park and we're camped at Willow River, a sweeping sand beach notorious for its "problem" black bears. This one fits the description, and people start to panic when he shows no sign of fear. By perfect coincidence, our trip is occurring a week after staff have received their annual bear training session. "This isn't a bear encounter," screams the staff supervisor, "this is a bear *incident!*" Another, the only other male in our group, takes on a more proactive approach. He becomes a raging caveman, banging pots and pans and tossing pieces of driftwood at the animal. The scene would be comical were it not for the waning daylight and the unimpressed, recalcitrant bear in our midst. He peers in every tent, nose high tuned for food.

With a mix of concern and curiosity, I allow the caveman to fire an aerial flare at the bear. I can't help but laugh when the fireball flies over the bruin's head and lands in the grass, starting a small brush fire. The bear is oblivious to the calamity unfolding around him. Then, as suddenly as he arrived, the bear disappears, likely having given up in his search for an easy meal. "We need a fire and we need people to stay up overnight," barks the supervisor, fresh off a two-way radio conversation with a park warden. "They won't come in to evacuate us in the dark, but with a fire the warden says we should be okay."

Clearly, the bear has moved on and I'd just as soon go to bed. But now all eyes are on me. Except for massive, tree-sized logs that have washed up onshore, the beach is devoid of the small wood park guidelines suggest we use for a "low-impact" campfire, and it's too dark for us to scour the forest. So I start dismantling the various pieces of arm- to leg-sized driftwood campers have assembled into furniture at this campsite over the years. "You can't burn *that*," says the supervisor.

"If you want an all-night fire," I respond, "just watch me."

Black bears are infrequently seen along Lake Superior's coastline. These fresh tracks crossed the beach at Picture Rock Harbour, just south of the Pukaskwa National Park Visitor Centre at Hattie Cove.

I pile the wood in the fire pit, splash it with stove fuel and toss in a match. Instantly the campsite is bathed in light. A few of us volunteer to take on the first watch around the fire and the supervisor promises that she will set her alarm for the second shift. We chat, tell stories, and scan the trees for bears lurking just beyond the firelight, but shortly after midnight the conversation slows and we're all ready to pack it in. As I head off to bed, I resist the urge to grunt and growl around the supervisor's tent. She doesn't wake up until eight the next morning.

"We need a woman to do this," says Mike Petzold, the owner of Caribou Expeditions, an outfitter based in Goulais River, north of Sault Ste. Marie. Together, Mike and I are guiding a group of eight sea kayakers in the Gargantua area of Lake Superior Provincial Park in late August, and now we've gathered our paddlers at Devil's Chair, a pyramid-shaped islet of volcanic rock deemed to be sacred by the Ojibwa.

One of our female paddlers scoots over and joins Mike at the base of the pillar, which viewed from one angle takes the form of an armchair, from another the profile of a reclining man with obscenely large genitals. "It is very important that you place your hand here," says Mike, "to appease this malevolent spirit."

The woman complies. Mike smiles and turns to the group. "She has touched the Devil's penis," he says. "This will ensure our safe passage."

His joke is strangely prescient. Combers sizzle on the outside of Devil's Chair, with two-metre swells rolling across hundreds of kilometres of open water from the northwest and crashing violently on the rock. I cast my best "are you sure you want to do this?" glance at Mike. He ignores me, and we exit the calm sheltered waters of Tugboat Channel and attempt to round rugged Cape Gargantua. The waves build, and soon water is rebounding off the cliff and creating a chaotic mess of whitecapped waves that stand taller than me.

There's no way I'd normally take clients out into these kinds of conditions, but with Mike along, I figure what the hell. There's something about the way Mike paddles that inspires confidence. It might be as simple as his posture in the boat, the latent power of his broad shoulders, the way his kayak surges forward with each stroke or how he's able to smile and maintain relaxed conversation in the roughest of seas. Once, paddling in late fall with friends, I watched him get lifted by a surging wave and deposited atop a rock cliff, several metres above the water. He exited his boat and assessed the situation. I watched in awe as he casually tossed the empty boat into the lake, dove in, and lithely re-entered his kayak in the tumultuous waves.

Most of our clients were rank beginners when they began the trip, but now, on Day Three, they are holding their own in conditions that would have most advanced kayakers shorebound. Afterward, Mike responds with trademark calm when I question his decision to lead the group into big, risky water. "They paid for a sea-kayaking trip," he says. "So that's what we have to give them."

Max paddles like he has something to prove. And since he came to vacation in Canada from his native Germany, is practically twice the age of the rest of the participants, and recently recovered from prostate cancer, maybe he does. He signed up for five consecutive weeklong guided trips on Lake Superior's north shore, from the Ontario-Minnesota border to the town of Wawa — an impressive six hundred kilometres of wilderness sea-kayaking. We conceived a series of seven back-to-back trips traversing the entire Canadian shore to inspire trophy hunters like Max to make segments of the "Big One" an annual event and generate return business. By dividing the route into seven-day segments, guides and clients could be swapped in and out and provisions resupplied at regular intervals.

Max is great to paddle with — so long as the rest of the group is compliant with his breakneck pace, advanced skills, and lack of patience for those with lesser ability and differing objectives. As luck would have it, I am responsible for guiding him for three legs of the trip. We have our first disagreement on Week One, when a marginal forecast of large waves and thunderstorms forces my decision to hole up on a cobblestone beach on an island west of Thunder Bay. Max has his tent taken down at the crack of dawn and his boat packed as I emerge from my tent and set about making breakfast. "Max, the forecast is bad," I tell him. "We're not going anywhere today." He looks at me with a combination of confusion and anger. "It's supposed to get rough," I explain. "You might as well unpack your boat and relax."

Instead, Max paces.

Three days later, we're ahead of schedule. We base camp on the tip of the Sibley Peninsula, and Max joins me on a hike up to the crest of the Sleeping Giant, a three-hundred-metre monolith of sedimentary rock overlooking

Thunder Bay. As we walk, I feel a twinge of regret for the way I've been impatient with Max. He's a genuinely nice guy, if a little Type A. Our brisk walk to the top of the Giant is an invigorating break from the usual slow pace of guided trips. He tells me about growing up in Nazi Germany, of barely surviving Allied bombardments and the freedom that came with the end of the Second World War. We sit for an hour at the summit and Max explains how surviving cancer has inspired his trips, and his desire to make each adventure meaningful because it could be his last. I hope I could be as vigorous as he is at age seventy-two.

On the second leg of the trip, Max is in his element when we're forced to put in several big days early on to avoid being stranded by an impending storm. He coaches some of the more novice members of our group in paddle strokes and techniques for dealing with headwinds. But after paddling one hundred kilometres in barely four days, even Max is ready for a break. The weather forecast is questionable and I make the call to take a layover on St. Joe Island, a long day's paddle from our resupply and switchover point in the village of Rossport. The storm hits in the late afternoon, lashing our campsite with a deluge of rain, intense thunder, and building waves.

When we're windbound a second day, still pinned down by twenty-five-knot winds, Max becomes antsy, and so do I. The forecast is dire — three- to four-metre waves for the next day and a half. Max rallies behind my decision to pack up on our third morning on St. Joe, in spite of the gusty, near-gale-force winds that buffet the channel we must cross. We take to the water and the group promptly scatters before the wind. I pull the plug immediately and organize a crash landing on a beach scarcely a kilometre from our last camp-site. Then I head out on the water to assess our options. I meet up with a large trawler whose captain offers to shuttle us back to the docks in Rossport. After today's brief, hair-raising paddle, most of the group realizes that it's our only chance to get out on time, and all I want to do is get home. When I tell him it's time to load up, Max shakes his head and resists like a stubborn teenager. He equates the boat ride with failure. He's despondent and silent on the bouncy, three-hour passage.

"There's nothing different from these people and the kids at summer camp," whispers my co-guide, Heidi. "Only they're older and have more money."

Heidi is fed up with Stan, who is another one of the many Max archetypes who sign up for guided trips. He's persistent and pestering to run every whitewater rapid on the White River. So far we've allowed him and his partner to canoe some of the easier rapids, but now he's pushing to go bigger. We give in, and watch Stan take a pinball course down the rapid, his canoe filling with water, bouncing off rocks, and nearly capsizing.

There's a common thread running between every close call I've had: some sort of premonition or bad feeling foreshadowing a looming disaster. An hour before the tandem kayak capsize incident, we stopped for lunch in a beautiful sandy cove. The sun was shining, the breeze rustling through the treetops, and the lake lapping on the shore. It would've been a perfect place to camp; I almost made the call. Instead, we got back on the water.

When leading a group of inexperienced paddlers on the open water of Lake Superior or a flooding whitewater river, it sometimes feels like you're tiptoeing on the back of a dragon. I've pulled into a sheltered cove after an hour of exposed paddling only to have an intense thunderstorm hit moments after we touched the beach. More times than I can remember have I taken novice sea kayakers in two-metre waves, taking bold risks in big, cold water to finish a trip on time. True, I have advanced paddling skills and have practised many contrived rescue scenarios in rough water, but there's a certain unpredictability when accidents unfold in real life. I've seen canoes wallow in grabby hydraulics on the Agawa River, gunwales inches from the water. On the first trip I guided alone, I was forced to land a group of novices through metre-high surf on a sandy beach, and watched three out of five kayaks upset, their occupants emerging shocked and panicked. At some point it's inevitable the dragon catches us off guard.

At the end of just about every summer of guiding, I've wondered if it's something I'll come back to do again the next year. It was a dream job initially, with my only reservation being the lacklustre pay, which was never enough to fund the next eight months at university. Then, slowly, I began to lose patience for the guests — their general ineptitude and the associated risks and responsibility, their pushiness and lack of respect, their innocence of the inherent dangers of wilderness travel. I grew to dislike (sometimes even hate) the stress of preparing and cooking gourmet meals for groups after a long day on the water.

Winter has a way to tempering these frustrations, and for the past few years I've struck a happy balance of leading more experienced groups of paddlers who supply their own gear and cook for themselves. I play the role of expedition leader, decision-maker, nature interpreter, and storyteller. For the most part it's a great gig, better still when my inner voice of experience speaks up and saves me from a jam. Since the close call with the tandem kayak at the mouth of the White River, I've learned to listen to my gut.

There wasn't space on the rescue boat for all our gear that late afternoon, so I offered to paddle my kayak and tow the tandem the eight kilometres back to park headquarters. But first I let the heat of the wave-sculpted rocks soothe my nerves and dropped a healthy pinch of sweet-smelling tobacco into the water as an offering of thanksgiving to the lake. After a long, rejuvenating while, I paddled off into the sunset.

CHAPTER 12

Salvage Rights

Years ago, writer Edward Abbey fathered a radical environmental movement with the fictional account of George Washington Hayduke, a man who sought to blow up the Colorado River's monstrous Glen Canyon Dam. The Monkey Wrench Gang *was the bestselling product of Abbey's experience paddling amid the sandstone arches of the pulsing waterway that has been buried beneath the stagnant waters of Lake Powell since 1963. Abbey, alongside pioneering eco-crusader David Brower of the Sierra Club and later the Friends of the Earth and Colorado River guide Martin Litton, sparked a generation of river conservationists and paddlers, the likes of whom have fought to preserve whitewater from the American West to northern Quebec.*

There's something morose about writing a requiem for a wild river. In the case of the White River, a Lake Superior tributary that was recently dammed and diverted for hydroelectric generation, maybe it's this depressing element that caused me to delay my final canoe trip on it to the very last minute, mere days before its awe-inspiring Umbata Falls was silenced and rerouted to a generator building. On a bittersweet trip like this it was impossible not to experience first-hand the magnitude of one of Brower's greatest tenets: We cannot recreate wilderness; once it's lost, it's gone forever. To be the last to experience a wild landscape gave new meaning to the challenges and heartbreaks of conservation.

Indeed, the story of the White River is one of compromise. On one hand, it is only fair that two local First Nation communities have the right to develop it for water power and the associated economic benefits. As it happens, these privileges were awarded before the White River was designated as a provincial waterway park, which ostensibly should've protected it from such developments. Even with the hulking Umbata Dam and the environmental degradation that goes along with it, the White River is still a worthwhile canoe trip. It's just like how diehard whitewater paddlers still line up for years in the lottery for permits to paddle the remaining section of wild Colorado River below the Glen Canyon Dam. But to have canoed it in its wild state is to realize that the new White River is a tamer, less fulfilling experience that's more of the sort that modern-day adventurers have come to expect. In allowing it to be to be sacrificed for economic development, we have committed one of river guide Litton's cardinal sins: we've made a compromise in a special place where finding the middle ground only amounts to conceding defeat. We've lost something timeless that, intrinsically, is worth more than all the electrical generating capacity in the world.

On a river in the boreal forest of northwestern Ontario, I'm thinking about the American Southwest. In the late 1950s, legendary writer Edward Abbey took a final raft trip down the wild Glen Canyon, just before a dam closed the Colorado River in 1963 and formed placid, sterile Lake Powell in its wake. Abbey immortalized the paradisiacal Canyonlands in his essays and spawned the "radical environmental movement" with *The Monkey Wrench Gang*, a novel published in 1975 in which protagonist George Washington Hayduke plots to blow up the Glen Canyon Dam.

The White River flows into Lake Superior just east of the northern Ontario town of Marathon, at the north end of Pukaskwa National Park. It drains a huge (by Lake Superior standards) watershed, rising near the town of White River on the Trans-Canada Highway and flowing over two hundred kilometres to its mouth on Lake Superior. With countless exciting rapids and several walleye-laden lakes along its course, the river is cherished by canoeists and anglers alike. As an added bonus for paddlers, it's one of the few whitewater rivers feeding into Lake Superior that can be descended throughout the paddling season, even in dry years.

But the White suffered a similar fate to Abbey's Colorado — albeit on a smaller scale. I first paddled it nearly a decade ago, when the threat of hydro-electric development along its course was mere hearsay. My friend Chris delayed our departure when he stumbled upon a fresh roadkill moose near his home in Wawa and spent a frenzied eighteen-hour session in his garage butchering his prize with a frightening assortment of chainsaws and knives. Then, with a sizeable supply of fresh moose meat weighing down our food pack, we loaded our canoe and set off on our early June trip. There were countless exciting rapids, cascading falls, and calm meanders interspersed with a healthy number of portages and classic Canadian Shield granite and sand campsites. We fried steaks in cast iron over crackling campfires, swam in the tannin-stained pools beneath, and tied T-shirts around our necks and heads for respite from the insatiable bugs.

The highlight of the trip was Umbata Falls, where Chris and I ignored the modern portage that makes use of a recent logging road and instead white-knuckled our way into an eddy at the brink of the waterfall, deafened by the roar of the thirty-metre drop. From there we sniffed out a trail, shouldered our gear, and followed an ancient, faintly marked, ankle-twisting portage, earning slack-jaw views from the rim of the billowing canyon. Chris shared his conspiracy theory that rerouting the scenic, traditional portage to the boring, three-kilometre death march on the road that's used by most river travellers was a means of keeping conservation-oriented canoeists from viewing the falls. In other words, the road served to keep the Haydukes of the world in a state of ignorant bliss — and to offer hydroelectric developers easy access to the falls.

Downstream, the White makes another five sizeable plunges to Lake Superior, but none are quite as spectacular as Umbata. On my first trip down the river we spent our last night camped at the mouth, enamoured by a week spent on a wild river and not looking forward to returning to civilization at dawn.

A veil of water tumbles from the brink of Umbata Falls, a thirty-metre cascade on the White River, just outside of Pukaskwa National Park's northwestern boundary. The falls was harnessed for hydroelectricity in 2008.

• • •

I vowed to never paddle the White River again when I learned in 2003 that the local Pic River Ojibwa band had partnered with a southern Ontario developer to build a dam and hydroelectric generating station at Umbata. The proposed project had a rated generating capacity of twenty-three megawatts, approximately the amount of energy needed to power six thousand homes. It was approved in spite of the White's 1999 designation as a provincial water-way park. The government's position was that it was obliged to keep a 1993 promise to reserve Umbata and two other falls on the river for hydro power.

Curiosity eventually led me to the developer's website, which showed aerial photos with schematic overlays of rubber weirs, impoundment areas, and an underground penstock that would burrow through bedrock beneath the old portage trail and channel the river's flow into twin turbines. A dam at the top of the main thirty-metre falls would create a headpond upstream, effectively drowning out the spectacular canyon Chris and I paddled to access the portage. I was enraged and wrote a lengthy, passionate letter to my Member of Provincial Parliament. The stock reply I received in return signified the White's fate; my concerns were too little, too late.

During the construction phase of the development, canoeists were offered an olive branch in the form of an all-terrain vehicle shuttle around the dam site, eliminating the once-gruelling portage. The company promised to develop a "campground" at Umbata Falls and to continue to service canoeists with a motorized shuttle that carefully avoided the newly industrialized land-scape. The need for these services was ostensibly gleaned from a survey that water-power officials conducted to poll the opinions of canoeists on the river. More likely they are only signs of the times, a sanitation of the wilderness.

Countless smaller, "run-of-the-river" projects like Umbata, and larger, Hydro Quebec–style mega-developments could become even more common on Canada's rivers in the years to come. It's mostly a matter of politics — the Ontario provincial government has pledged to shut down coal-powered gen-erating stations and the federal Transport Canada agency managed to gut the provisions of the Navigable Waters Protection Act, effectively opening the flood-gates for developments on rivers from coast to coast.

Today, there's a battle for wild rivers in British Columbia, where an aggres-sive government policy aimed at exporting vast quantities of hydroelectricity has created a claim-staking rush for developers, with over six hundred rivers subject to proposals. Meanwhile, Quebec premier Jean Charest has made a vast network of dams, reservoirs, and rerouted rivers in the northern part of the province — the next phase of the ongoing James Bay Project — a key item in his political legacy. The first incarnation of the project in the 1970s uprooted Aboriginal people, flooded vast areas with stagnant reservoirs, and released the neurotoxin methyl mercury into the environment, which in turn entered the food chain, poisoning fish, birds, and humans. In Ontario, the wild, one-thousand-kilometre-long Albany River and hosts of smaller waterways are subject to pending hydroelectric development in the decades to come.

Even the staunchest river advocate will admit that hydro power imposes fewer climate change–inducing impacts than burning coal or natural gas. It's true that in the age of global warming, harnessing the emissions-free energy of falling water sounds like a logical, "made in Canada" way to meet electricity needs. But environmentalists like Janet Sumner, the executive director of the Canadian Parks and Wilderness Society's Wildlands League Ontario chapter, argue that feeding the grid with more hydroelectricity does nothing to curb our swelling appetite for power.

So-called run-of-the-river projects may not create sprawling, Lake Powell–like storage reservoirs, but in many places they still represent the industrialization of untouched wilderness. The fossil fuel–intensive dam-building process involves helicopters, bulldozers, dynamite, hundreds of kilometres of new roads and transmission corridors, and thousands of tons of steel and cement. There are also ecological impacts associated with altered flow rates on aquatic environments, clear-cuts, and habitat fragmentation due to access roads. And then there's the physics of shipping hydroelectricity from the hinterlands to Canada's populous core — megawatts of energy are lost when power is wired long distances. It's clear that hydro-power catchwords like "green," "environmentally friendly," and "renewable" don't justify the loss of some of Canada's finest wilderness rivers.

It's ironic that in parts of North America there's a growing movement to return rivers to a more natural state. According to conservation organization American Rivers, based in Washington, D.C., 306 obsolete or environmentally destructive dams were removed between 1999 and 2008. It seems U.S. engineers have learned lessons from previous projects and are choosing to squeeze extra megawatts of power out of existing developments with technological improvements rather than building new facilities.

There are even compelling arguments justifying Hayduke's goal of demolishing the Glen Canyon Dam, whose turbines have slowed due to silt buildup and growing demand for water in the American Southwest. The accumulation of sediments that occurs when a river is imprisoned by a buttress of concrete and steel is a dam's Achilles heel. Eventually, all reservoirs, from the sprawling human-made lakes of northern Quebec to the relatively small retention area of the Umbata Falls Dam, will fill with silt. At some point, turbines stop spinning and the dam fails. In the case of mega-projects, there are instances where the sheer weight of wet mud (which has approximately twice the mass of water alone) has advanced the timing of seismic events, such as a devastating earthquake in China's Sichuan province in May 2008 that killed seventy thousand people. It's likely no coincidence that the geological fault line that slipped was adjacent to a huge dam and reservoir.

When asked about the ticking time bomb of sedimentation looming in Lake Powell, longtime United States Bureau of Reclamation head Floyd Dominy replied, "We will let the people of the future worry about it." But a perfect storm of climate change — namely reduced precipitation and increasing surface water evaporation — and a skyrocketing demand for fresh water in the parched American Southwest has dropped Lake Powell levels by two-thirds between 1999 and 2005; at this rate, some physicists, including James Powell, a geologist, author, and the executive director of the United States National Physical Science Consortium, believe that it could be a mud flat in less than fifty-five years, clogging the outflow feeding into the Grand Canyon. This will have untold consequences on a huge swath of land — ecological effects downstream when the Colorado River runs dry, power shortages, and the apocalyptic flood that would result if the Glen Canyon Dam failed beneath seventy billion tons of mud. Indeed, Dominy's moment of reckoning is coming far sooner than he ever expected.

It's true that smaller installations like the Umbata Falls Dam don't impose the same level of social, economic, and environmental risk as mega-projects. And in many ways it can be argued that the minimal direct carbon emissions of hydroelectricity make it a better alternative to coal or natural gas. But there's an ethical question to consider as developers rush to stake the last flowing rivers. Asks Sumner, "Do we really want to be in the position where we've dammed all of our rivers?"

• • •

To grapple with this question, I gave in to curiosity and decided to retrace the trip I did years ago with my friend Chris. In the spirit of "salvage tourism" — like Abbey on the Colorado or the growing list of adventurers racing to be the last to see landscapes imperiled by climate change, mineral development, and urban sprawl — I asked my wife, Kim, to join me on a final run on the White River. As it happened, we timed our trip merely a few days before the river's flow was shunted and Umbata's powerhouse turbines spun for the first time.

The first few days of the eighty-five-kilometre-long trip were much the way I remembered it. We hoot and holler through chutes of whitewater, sneak by a moose with a platter-sized rack in a backwater lagoon, catch a momentary glimpse of a wolf, and examine a beaver dam stretching several hundred metres — one of the longest we've ever seen. Our nights are spent in the shelter of copses of boreal spruce and cedar. Despite the fact that it's October, the river is still warm enough for Kim and I to take a few swims to cool off after the portages. Kim enthuses about the river's mix of challenging whitewater, scenic falls, and biologically diverse backwater pools. I'm more cautious with my optimism, but with the exception of a few obnoxious ribbons of orange flagging tape marking two other potential hydro sites that the Ontario Ministry of Natural Resources has issued to another First Nation, I saw nothing calling for Hayduke-like ecotage.

We reach Umbata at lunch on Day Three. Whereas Chris and I tiptoed our way through the dark and mysterious canyon, Kim and I have no choice but to take on the long portage on the road. And since recreational canoeing season is long since over, there's no all-terrain vehicle to Sherpa our loads. The upshot of this is that are also no company officials on hand to smooth over the development's environmental scars with practised rhetoric and mask from the fact that the impacts of dam building go far beyond dried-up rapids and flooded forests. I brace myself to see the raw effects of the development.

Later on, Pic River economic development official Byron LeClair tells me how successful his band has been with its previous hydroelectric project on the nearby Black River — how the Cree of northern Quebec are relying on Pic River's experiences in harnessing the power of rivers in their territory for rich economic rewards. There's no doubt LeClair is walking a fine line in balancing his cultural heritage with the economic realities of the modern

A memorial was erected at Chicagonce Falls for a whitewater kayaker who drowned there in the spring of 1975. The ten-metre falls is the subject of another water-power proposal on the White River.

world. When he's finished boasting about the dams, he recounts a story about his canoe trip last summer to harvest wild rice and announces his plans to vote for the Green Party in the next election.

But LeClair's honourable opinions are far from my mind as I carry the canoe on a road that passes through clear-cuts, transmission corridors reeking of chemical pesticides, and mounds of pulverized bedrock. The old logging road has been improved to handle the traffic of heavy machinery, and with it has come piles of discarded Tim Hortons coffee cups, potato-chip bags, and cigarette cartons.

Descending the final grade to the river, with the canoe weighing heavily on my shoulders, I sense something more symbolic. A thin veil of poplar barely hides bedrock cliffs that have been blasted apart to provide space for a box store-sized generating structure. Behind it, the ominous maw of the once-roiling, rockbound river downstream of the falls is diminished. To be sure, LeClair's talk of economic independence for Canadian First Nations has credence, but on this day I can't help but think about the belief among some elders that the spirits of the dead rise in the mist above a waterfall. It feels like we're witnessing the dying breaths of the spirit of the White River.

Ultimately, I know have no right to this river or this land, but that doesn't separate it from my heart. My eyes well with tears and I want to erupt — to attack the monstrous powerhouse with obscenities and rocks. I think about the other wild rivers that have been lost in the last century, of the rock canyons of the Kaministiquia, Michipicoten, Magpie, and Montreal — the Glen Canyons of the Lake Superior basin, long silenced. I wonder if the new dam on the White River will set a precedent for more; the thought makes me sick.

"Freedom, not safety, is the highest good," said George Washington Hayduke, Edward Abbey's fictional alter ego. But it's too late to fight for the White's freedom, and I can't stand to stick around. There's no satisfaction in salvage tourism; no sense of accomplishment in being the final person to paddle the White River before turbines spin, power lines hum, and Umbata runs dry. One day, the negligible amount of power produced could easily be saved through conservation. What good is a dam when there's no demand for power? Faraway, in the American Southwest, it's sadly ironic that Abbey's beloved Canyonlands have in parts reappeared, as Lake Powell levels continue to drop to feed thirsty desert metropolises and the Glen Canyon Dam stands high, dry, and increasingly strained by a mass of mud.

Pic River First Nation's Umbata Falls generating facility produces approximately twenty-three megawatts of electricity, enough to power around six thousand homes. A dam at the top of the falls creates a small headpond and reroutes water through a tunnel to the generator. When power is being produced, only a trickle of water flows through the canyon beneath Umbata Falls.

In my rage, I fail to tell Kim that the rapid immediately below the falls is one of the toughest on the river — a steep, fast-paced, and ferocious mess of waves and rocks. But on a day like this it feels good to throw caution into the wind. We load the canoe and run it blind, backpaddling, drawing, and crashing through waves and cleanly missing pillow-shaped rocks and the recirculating hydraulics that threaten to sink our humble ship. This time, there are no cries of joy and excitement. Downstream, the last wild breath of the White River beckons. We have no choice but to dig deep and go with the flow.

CHAPTER 13

Tales of an Empty Cabin

Like any backwoods area, the north shore of Lake Superior has plenty of abandoned cabins, ranging from rough-hewn, doghouse-sized trapline camps to elaborate log fishing lodges, like the tired old Bissineau establishments at Agawa Bay. All along the coast, the broken windows of these structures peer out at the lake emptily, their walls crumbling and slowly returning to the earth in heaps of rotting wood and crumbling tar. Up until fairly recently, a few could still be relied upon for emergency shelter: The roof finally gave way on the old Mills-Fletcher cabin at remote Pukaskwa Depot, a 1920s logging camp at the south end of Pukaskwa National Park, a little more than a decade ago; and the sixty-year-old General Motors executive retreat on Old Woman Lake, just inland from Lake Superior, is still used to escape the rain by the odd canoe tripper.

It's always exciting to find signs of human life deep in the wilderness. There's something about experiencing the dreams of others, catching a glimpse of how they lived, and imagining their response to the rugged landscape that transcends adventurous spirits. My friend Jorma Paloniemi finds particular pleasure in discovering these old haunts in the backwoods, and, like a twelve-year-old playing fort in the backyard, conjuring up ways in which these long-forgotten structures can be remodelled for another use.

Of course, most of these old cabins are too filled with bat and mouse droppings, too leaky or too rotted to even consider using, but sometimes you get lucky. Such was the case years ago when Jorma stumbled upon a small cabin hidden behind a veil of cedars on a remote lake north of Lake Superior's Batchawana Bay. Despite years of abandonment, the place was still usable; Jorma just needed to find some hardy, backcountry skiing friends keen to share it with him. In another stroke of luck, he met Lorraine. The cabin became their ski chalet, tucked in an undeveloped oasis of ponds and hills north of Sault Ste. Marie.

• • •

We decide that our friend Jorma Paloniemi must be a reincarnated river otter shortly after we ski across the first ice-covered lake and enter a thick, unkempt forest. Only a slick and powerful weasel could penetrate brush this thick. Our route to this point has been easy, up a long, two-hundred-metre incline along five kilometres of hard-packed snowmobile trail. But now the snowmobile tracks have petered out and have been replaced by waist-deep snowdrifts as we head off into the unknown, skiing a forty-five-degree compass bearing through the screen of trees, aiming for another lake across a kilometre of rugged terrain. It doesn't take us long to find the smooth furrow of an otter, gliding on a greasy belly through the forest from one lake to the next. The track follows our compass course precisely. Barely discernable beneath the otter slide are the twin ski tracks Jorma laid down when he skied this way nearly a month before.

My wife Kim and I look at each other and smile. We are going it alone, following our friend's sketchy directions to a hidden cabin in the Algoma hills, high above Lake Superior's Batchawana Bay. Jorma and his partner, Lorraine, call the rough-hewn twelve-by-twelve-foot vertical log camp "Dodger" because they suspect that it was once the hideout of a Vietnam draft resister. The prospect of venturing across unknown country is intimidating, but at least we have an ally in a route-finding otter.

Jorma has spent most of his life exploring these hills on foot, booting around the old logging roads on a dirt bike, snorkelling the lakes, and revisiting the same country by snowmobile and cross-country ski in the winter. He discovered Dodger and several other cabins on these oft solo missions, shelters tucked away and long forgotten in terrain that's virtually impenetrable for much of the year — deep swamps, beneath the sweeping canopies of cedar, and amidst cube van–sized rocks atop rugged hills. Most of the buildings he found were tiny — "about the size of a doghouse," he said — and constructed of axe-hewn cedar.

He remembered a story about draft dodgers hiding out in the area, supported by local sympathizers who tossed bundles of groceries over the highway shoulders in winter storms to conceal their tracks. Trouble is, he can't remember where he'd heard this theory — it could've been from a backhoe operator from Jones Landing, a once-bustling logging hamlet below the hills on the shore of Lake Superior, now a cluster of houses and junkyards beside the Trans-Canada Highway, or maybe from outdoor adventurer and professional photographer Gary McGuffin.

It took Jorma the better part of forty years to find a partner as compliant and adventurous as Lorraine. He wasn't expecting much out of the old cabin five years ago when he took Lorraine for her first chance to see it; he thought they might find an intact roof if they were lucky, otherwise a heap of old rotting logs, a dump of rusted fuel and beer cans, and scads of abandoned bedding and clothing. When they got there after navigating a rough logging road by Jeep and skiing a few kilometres over a series of frozen lakes, they found the garbage they anticipated, but also a surprisingly livable camp for something that had clearly been abandoned for years. They set to burning what garbage they could, swept out the building, inventoried its useable contents — mostly old dishes and silverware, pots and pans, shovels and axes — and started to dream up the backcountry skiing routes they could stage, using Dodger as an outpost chalet.

As Kim and I hit the second lake, we're immediately taken by the winter paradise that Jorma has uncovered. The region looks lacklustre on the maps: a collection of unnamed ponds, swamps, and old and new logging roads, decent topography, but no named peaks. But if you look closer, especially if you're a backcountry skier, you'll notice that the area supports natural travel corridors that are predominantly over frozen water — the easiest type of skiing — with few overland portions and thus minimal exposure to dreaded "shnarb," the tangled messes of alder swales and young maples that haunt the dreams of winter travellers.

We're enjoying glorious spring skiing — the air temperature hovers just below freezing and the sky is a rich blue. The late-March snow is crusty and fast on the lakes, and the "portages" become markedly easier once we discover the otter — and Jorma's — path of least resistance. As the buffer grows between us and the logging roads, so does the girth of the trees. By the time we reach the third lake we're gawking up at ten-storey-tall old growth white pine and making tracks through mature maples between the lakes.

Jorma has marked the Dodger cabin with an *X* on our topographic map, on the tip of a vaguely boot-shaped point on an unnamed lake that measures about a kilometre long. After five hours we're certain that we've found the right lake; all matches up on the map except for the fact that we can't find the cabin. We troll the shoreline, eying the thick screen of balsam and cedar: Nothing. We look nervously at the sun and our watches. It's been a beautiful day of skiing so far, but we both know it would be a death march if we had to bail out, retrace our tracks, and race the sunset back to the highway. Just as we're about to turn tail and beat a hasty retreat, Kim spots a glint of glass. We awkwardly sidestep up the bank and crash through the trees.

The "Dodger" cabin is hidden amongst mature eastern white cedar trees on a small, unnamed lake in the hills east of Lake Superior's Batchawana Bay.

It's just the place to hide and not be found. The graying old cabin is blanketed in snow, obscured by the branches of a massive leaning cedar. Its window is dark, its door latched with a fork.

The evidence kept piling up in support of Jorma's Vietnam draft dodger theory: An old, decomposing newspaper in the camp was dated 1970, about the same time as the long-fought war; the camp was proximal to the U.S.-Canada border at Sault Ste. Marie; and it was heated with a woodstove and spacious enough to support a person or two for an extended stay. But after our adventures in finding the place, I was tempted to believe it served a parallel purpose for a different kind of occupant.

I first heard about "tripwire veterans" in *Halfway Man,* a novel set on Lake Superior by the late Wayland Drew. Though a work of fiction, I believe Drew weaved some facts into the novel. For starters, he knew the north shore well, primarily from the seat of a canoe, and anyone familiar with Lake Superior on similar terms can recognize real-life landmarks in Drew's fiction. What's more, he also authored *Superior: The Haunted Shore,* a definitive work of non-fiction about the place.

So when he describes Travis Niskigwun, *Halfway Man's* main character, and his brother Cutler's run-in with a hardened Vietnam militiaman running scared of society and hiding out in a fortified cabin on Lake Superior's north shore, I tend to believe that tripwire vets might've truly existed. The notion cuts against the grain of the image of wispy hippies who chose to resist the draft, crossed the border to Canada, and escaped to communes in the lotus lands of British Columbia. Rather, these were war veterans, likely suffering from post-traumatic stress disorder. "Some Vietnam veterans could *feel* people getting close, as if their skin had grown special sensors," Drew wrote in *Halfway Man*:

> They had to be away from the crowds, away from the streets, back in the bush. Way back. A few went up into Oregon, and northern Washington, and British Columbia. A few came across the Lake.
>
> Twice when we were boys Cutler and I found abandoned boats — tanks, motor, everything — swamped and half-buried on beaches east of Neyashing. They were old

battered things that guys had bought for next to nothing somewhere on the south shore — Grand Marais, Duluth, Marquette — and had driven across on a fairly calm night. When they hit the beach they just kept going straight north, up toward the height of land and sometimes a long way beyond, I guess. Into the taiga. Into the tundra …

Batchawana Bay is an easy cross-border hop from Michigan, a reasonable twenty-five-kilometre water crossing at the most. I imagined the person who built this cabin stealing across from Whitefish Point on the American side, landing on the sand beach at Havilland or Harmony, north of Sault Ste. Marie, and hitting the ground running. Building supplies could've been salvaged from one of the many old logging camps in the area; in fact, Jorma maintains that the logs used to construct the Dodger cabin came from a horse-logging-era barn closer to Lake Superior.

A 1985 article by Larry Heinemann in *Harper's* magazine examines the psychology of tripwire vets in greater detail. The term "tripwire" comes from a propensity to booby trap the perimeter of their hermitage with inconspicuous, blackened, fishing line–thin wire. Attached to some sort of noisemaker, Heinemann described this as a sort of "early warning system" like the "little hawk's bell a shopkeeper might attach to the front door of his place to announce customers."

Similarly, in *Halfway Man*, the bush-savvy Niskigwun brothers track a complex network of monofilament until they can see what's at its centre: A man bearing an assault rifle. "All those lines led in to him, each one tied to a finger or a toe, and by tensing them just a bit he could keep the perimeter line taut," wrote Drew. "He could sense twenty different places on it, like a spider in the centre of a web. The gun, that was for anything that touched that monofilament … He wasn't asleep but he wasn't awake, either. Something in between."

Heinemann portrays tripwire veterans as shell-shocked men who "just don't fit" into society. He argues against the image of "a mossbacked old hard-ass … just as squirrelly as hell and literally shivering with paranoia, who hops and whoops around those evergreen forests like some mangy, half-mad freak." Rather, Heinemann posits that escaping society was veterans' means of controlling their rage and angst and getting their lives back together. "Out there everything 'fits,' everything works; maybe they can too," writes Heinemann, quoting a Port Angeles, Washington, family counsellor. A combat veteran known simply as Steve the Bear tells Heinemann, "I knew there was a gentleness and a peacefulness with the animals that you never saw with humans. And that was what I needed to see. It was part of my healing. I desperately needed to know that there was still gentleness — that my whole world wasn't caving in completely."

If there ever was a place to make crooked nerves straight, this small lake high above Lake Superior is it. All is quiet as Kim and I make dinner, kindle a fire in the rusty, plate-steel woodstove and watch the shadows lengthen across the lake. It's hard to believe that we're less than a day's ski from the Trans-Canada Highway, just north of Sault Ste. Marie. This is a place where massive old-growth white pine and gnarly cedar still exist, the deep snow dotted with moose tracks, the air crisp and clean. It feels like we're far out in the wilderness, and the sensation of remoteness puts the mind at ease.

After my first visit, I discovered Heinemann's article, re-read Drew's novel, and started to build up the legend of Jorma's hidden ski chalet in my mind. In my imagination, the notion of shell-shocked veterans braving the open waters of Lake Superior to seek solace in the northern Ontario wilderness had an uncanny similarity to the Ojibwa story of Myeengun, the old-school militiaman believed to have led a canoe brigade of warriors across the heart of Lake Superior to thwart an Iroquois offensive three hundred years ago, as depicted in red ochre pictographs on granite cliffs just north of Agawa Bay.

For Jorma and Lorraine, though, the place was still Dodger (Tripwire didn't have the same ring, I suppose) and its purpose was less romantic and more utilitarian. While I enthused about my theories of the cabin's history, Jorma made plans for a late summer trip to install much-needed new roofing material. He scoped out the old logging roads and found a bone-rattler that would get us within a two-hour paddle of the cabin by kayak. Our friend Craig agreed to come along and we braved the long, uphill road in two trips — the first a Friday-night mission to haul a trailer-load of kayaks, hand tools, chainsaws, and a hulking roll of tarpaper to the log landing at the end of the road, and the second a cramped ride in Jorma's four-by-four pickup truck the next morning to start the adventure.

Hauling strange things in whitewater kayaks is familiar business for Jorma. In the early 1990s, he worked a trapline in the Algoma Highlands north of Sault Ste. Marie and hauled many a beaver carcass out of the bush by kayak. But for those more accustomed to the recreational aspects of paddling, hauling toolboxes and chainsaws over non-existent portages is a new, challenging, and quickly exhausting experience. Our tiny crafts are slow and sluggish across the lakes and equally bullish to drag through the bush. But for the most part the trip in goes as planned, giving us a better feel for the lay of the land and a chance to hash out new ski routes.

We're travelling primarily on old trails — the vestiges of two tracks still carved into the forest floor by the horse teams of the toughened men who once logged this forest with saws and axes decades ago. When mechanized logging took over in the 1950s and 1960s, many of these trails were plied by the big wheels of skidders, which replaced horses to drag cut logs out of the bush. Amazingly, much of the country is reforested and the complexity of the old road network is only apparent to keen eyes. What's more obvious, however, is how easy it would've been to get around back here when these old roads were in their prime, say thirty or forty years ago. It would have been nothing for a recluse to find a hidden patch of land back here, only to make easy, covert forays down to the highway and hitchhike south to Sault Ste. Marie when supplies ran low.

These thoughts flow through my mind has we cut and nail a new layer of tarpaper on the old cabin roof. We clean up inside and re-seal the log walls. We cut, split, and stack enough firewood to last several winters of regular visits. All that's left now is to wait for the snow.

Every trip to the Dodger cabin feels like a pilgrimage. It seems like a privilege to find its welcoming shelter after a challenging ski tour over sketchy December lake ice or through deep March snowdrifts. Once, my wife Kim and I joined Jorma and Lorraine to spend New Year's Eve at the cabin. A brief post-Christmas thaw had made the usual route across the ponds too risky, so we travelled overland instead, crashing through tangles of alder and balsam fir and seeking out the easier routes on the ridges. We finally arrived near sunset, and set about re-rigging the stovepipe with our icy fingers as the temperature plummeted. Once fixed and lit, the stove promptly warmed the cabin and we celebrated the arrival of 2009 in T-shirts.

After each visit, we schemed about the place's history. Then, finally, Jorma and I rustled up the courage to talk to the old-timer in the small Batchawana Bay community of Jones Landing who we thought might know the real story of Dodger cabin. When we met him on a blustery Sunday afternoon in late January, the retired heavy-machine operator seemed unsure of our motives, setting the tone for an awkward encounter. Jorma tried to set his mind at ease with small talk, but to no avail. The brief conversation took place in the man's dark, cold, and damp garage; we later laughed that he was too uncomfortable with our bizarre inquiries to let us in his house.

Lorraine Wakely dines by candlelight inside the small twelve-by-twelve-foot cabin. Heated by woodstove, the cabin is quick to warm to T-shirt temperatures.

What we got was this: at some point, likely during the Second World War, a steelworker from Sault Ste. Marie, Ontario, escaped the Allied draft by hiding out in a cabin in the hills north of Batchawana Bay. He may or may not have been supported by sympathizers from the old farms that once supplied hay for the horse-loggers. His cabin was reasonably closer to Lake Superior than the one we'd appropriated, and by now had most likely decomposed back to the earth. The man showed us a dog-eared photo of the log camp, which was about twice the size of Dodger and in far worse condition, taken in the 1980s.

"But there's another cabin up there," Jorma pressed. "It's way back. I remember seeing it when I used to hunt up there."

"Oh, that one," replied the old timer with little hesitation. "Vertical log? Further back and just beyond the last of the old roads?"

Jorma nodded, then glanced at me and winked.

"That was an old moose-hunting camp," he said. "Some guys built it maybe forty years ago. There's probably nothing left of it now, either."

We didn't let on that we knew better, that the old cabin was still standing, recently re-roofed and well-used by a new generation of outdoor adventurers. Instead, we thanked the man and quietly took our leave from Jones Landing, retreating to an old motel bar just down the highway. We were the only ones in the place, sitting on stools, sipping beer and looking out at the squalls racing across Batchawana Bay. I was disheartened by the revelation that our hidden ski chalet was just a reclaimed hunt camp. But not Jorma: The news of another, unknown cabin to rediscover had kindled new plans.

"So there's still a Dodger camp back up there. It's just not ours," he said. "I wonder what's left of the original cabin he mentioned? I wonder if it's still there?" His eyes widened in excitement and, for a moment, his round face seemed to take on the mischievous look of an otter. "Do you want to try to find it?"

CHAPTER 14

Counting Caribou

It seems like a rite of passage for every environmental journalist to join biologists in a helicopter and take to the air in search of wildlife. I got my chance when I was lucky enough to fly with Pukaskwa National Park ecologist Martha Allen on a woodland caribou survey. We spent two hours in the air flying grid lines in the north end of the park, near the town of Marathon. Based on the horror stories I'd heard beforehand, I decided to pre-medicate with three motion-sickness tablets before we took off. Other than the warm, fuzzy feeling of sedative-induced sleepiness, I don't remember much about the flight, other than the fact that we saw no caribou and two moose. The survey was promptly called off and we were whisked back to the Marathon airport when one of Allen's assistants became nauseous and started to vomit.

It's believed that two hundred woodland caribou once roamed Pukaskwa National Park, but backcountry visitors are hard-pressed to spot a woodland caribou on a backpacking trip along Pukaskwa's sixty-kilometre-long Coastal Trail or a weeklong paddling trip down the shoreline today. Still, there are other places along Lake Superior's north shore where woodland caribou sightings are all but guaranteed. A population of one hundred to six hundred caribou booms and busts according to browse availability on the Slate Islands, a doughnut-shaped archipelago located ten kilometres offshore from Terrace Bay. And the estimated two-hundred-head herd on remote Michipicoten Island is a wildlife recovery success story, the product of a translocation of a small population of Slate Island caribou in the early 1980s. By visual appearance alone, the Michipicoten Island population appears to be healthy and vibrant.

Ultimately, the entire human population faces tough challenges when it comes to assisting with the long-term survival of endangered species. This is a symptom of a new era of environmentalism — the "End of Nature" described by U.S. environmental journalist and activist Bill McKibben. While governments squabble about short-term costs of research and recovery plans and how they influence their chances of re-election, the greater life-supporting implications of the simple presence of species *like woodland caribou often go ignored. Canada's boreal forest is a woodland-caribou stronghold and a critical global source of clean air and water — essential elements in maintaining all life on Earth. In fact, a comprehensive study by the Pembina Institute, a non-governmental environmental research and policy think tank, estimated the replacement value of the life-supporting services provided by Canada's boreal forest at $93 billion per year — more than twice the net return of natural resource extraction in the area. Politics aside, I think it's rather obvious that if we work to preserve woodland caribou habitat, we're also working to support ourselves.*

On a cold, windy, blue-sky day in late February, I get the melancholic feeling that I'm climbing aboard a mutant dragonfly with dire prophesies for the future of an icon of the Canadian wilderness. I've joined Parks Canada ecologist Martha Allen and two keen-eyed wildlife-spotting assistants for a helicopter survey of the backcountry of Pukaskwa National Park's north end. We're looking for the so-called grey ghosts of the boreal forest — woodland caribou, *Rangifer tarandus caribou*, an ungulate species closely related to Scandinavian reindeer. A small herd of these elusive animals is thought to still inhabit the mature black spruce, birch, and jack pine forests of Pukaskwa, an 1,800-square-kilometre reserve located on the Lake Superior coast south of Marathon.

This rockbound, lake-pocked wilderness used to be the heart of woodland caribou territory in Ontario, which extended as far south as Lake Nipissing, Algonquin Provincial Park, and, by some accounts, even the Oak Ridges Moraine on the outskirts of Toronto as recently as 1880. Since then, however, the province's woodland caribou population has plummeted. According to the Ontario Ministry of Natural Resources (MNR), caribou range has decreased by 50 percent across the province, declining at an average rate of nearly 35,000 square kilometres of territory per decade. As a result, the boreal population of the species is deemed "threatened" under Ontario's endangered species legislation and by Canada's Species at Risk Act.

Pukaskwa's holdout population is also believed to be in decline. When the park was formed in 1983, the region had an estimated thirty woodland caribou; at one time, before the boreal forest was turned into a patchwork of clear-cuts, pocked with gold mines and criss-crossed by forest access roads, biologists believe that it could have been home to as many as two hundred caribou. But

Woodland caribou are a common sight at the Slate Islands, a predator-free archipelago located ten kilometres offshore from the town of Terrace Bay. Being extremely strong swimmers, woodland caribou are thought to have populated the islands by swimming across from the mainland. Their population at the Slates booms and busts in cycles based on the availability of lichen, their preferred food source.

Parks Canada ecologist Martha Allen takes notes on a helicopter survey of historical wood-land caribou habitat in the north end of Pukaskwa National Park. Today, the majority of the park's estimated sixteen-animal herd is believed to live in the south end of the park, where Otter Island provides a refuge for calving females.

when I met her in the winter of 2009, Allen believed that the number was in the single digits. She was organizing a comprehensive survey using both the government's traditional "eye-spy" helicopter surveying method and a new, high-tech approach imported from the United States that uses fixed-wing aircraft and infrared detectors, which are able to detect and identify the unique "thermal signature" of radiation emitted by various types of animals, including woodland caribou, to get a more precise number. The goal is to get an exact population size for woodland caribou, not just a rough estimate from the helicopter, which is believed to have a success rate of only 50 percent.

The Bell Long Ranger chopper is buffeted by wind gusts as we lift off the tarmac at the Marathon Airport and head south, into park airspace. Following a global positioning system unit, the pilot manoeuvres the bird along a grid of three-kilometre-long flight lines, each separated by five hundred metres and a gut-whooping about-face. Inside, we press our faces against the cockpit windows, chat through headsets, and scan the snowy forest three hundred metres below. We sweep the coastal corridor traditionally inhabited by woodland caribou all the way to Adhik Lake, a tiny pond named after the Ojibwa word for caribou — "he that goes," referring to the 120-to-220-kilogram animals' incessant need to be on the move. But other than a pair of moose we spot wading belly-deep in snow, the flight is fruitless.

Allen is disappointed, but not surprised. To date, this year's helicopter surveys only revealed two woodland caribou and the tracks of a couple of others, observations all made in the more remote south end of the park. Still, she's hopeful for the plight of Pukaskwa caribou. "It sure feels like there's a lot of habitat here," she says. "There's a lot of undisturbed territory, and while there are wolf and moose populations [which act as predators and competitors, respectively], the coastal preferences of woodland caribou tend not to overlap with these species." Survey completed, headsets go silent as most of us battle the throes of nausea. Allen buries her head in her journal. Except for weather conditions and the details of our route, she has little good news to record as the chopper pilot beelines us back to the Marathon Airport.

At a conference over a decade ago, Dutch chemist, atmospheric scientist, and Nobel Prize winner Paul Crutzen candidly interrupted the chairman of the meeting to suggest that the Earth had entered a new geological era. We were no longer children of the Holocene, the epoch that began at the end of the last ice age, Crutzen implored, but rather a part of the "Anthropocene" — the age of man. Crutzen's colleagues jumped on the idea and encouraged him to elaborate on it. A 2002 article in the prestigious journal *Nature* followed, where the Dutch scientist described the new era as one defined by the massive, widespread impacts that rampant human activity have had on the planet's life-supporting systems, ranging from climate-altering changes to the atmosphere to terrestrial landscapes obliterated by agriculture, forestry, mining, and urbanization, to grossly contaminated oceans. Besides the physical impacts, perhaps the most telling feature of the Anthropocene is a looming epidemic of extinctions attributed to human activity.

Many scientists have now taken the Anthropocene as fact. Today, the debate isn't about the impacts of humans, but rather when the turning point of chronic effects first took hold. In his *Nature* article, Crutzen suggested the tide changed with the Industrial Revolution of the late eighteenth century, when humans first began spewing large amounts of carbon dioxide into the atmosphere. Others have argued that the shift came sooner, like the onset of agriculture eight thousand years ago. The observations of noted Harvard biologist E.O. Wilson imply it came with the post–Second World War baby boom, when the world's human population skyrocketed and so did rates of consumption. "The pattern of human population growth in the twentieth century was more bacterial than primate," wrote Wilson. That the combined biomass of the Earth's 7 billion humans is now estimated to be in the order of one hundred times larger than that of any other species that has inhabited the planet is a telling statistic in support of Wilson's view.

Currently, the Stratigraphy Commission of the Geological Society of London is debating whether or not to officially accept the Anthropocene as a formal unit of geological time. Regardless, the effects of humans on the natural environment cannot be denied. The big changes highlighted by Crutzen, whose key discoveries related to the ozone layer, are climatic — namely the phenomenon of human-induced global warming. Meanwhile, resource extraction, urban sprawl, and agriculture has mined out, cut down, paved over, and made monocultures of much of the planet's surface. The byproduct of these activities — various forms of pollution — has poisoned surface water and effectively turned the atmosphere into a greenhouse, imposing a dangerous feedback loop of warming temperatures.

The result has been sweeping losses in biological diversity around the world. Sensitive species like woodland caribou have been among the first to fall. Canada's barren-ground, or migratory, caribou and its slightly smaller, woodland-dwelling subspecies were once the nation's most common species of cervid (deer). Today, however, caribou are outnumbered by moose, white-tailed, and black-tailed deer, all of which are more tolerant of human development.

The reason is that, as a rule, all forms of caribou need vast, untrammelled areas in order to survive. In this regard, even the populous caribou of the Slate Islands are playing with a shortened deck. As noted in the Ojibwa name for the creature, caribou are the long-haul travellers of the animal world. In them, evolution has created the perfect energy-miser: per kilogram of body mass, a caribou has the lowest energy cost of movement of any terrestrial mammal, topping even the notorious roamers of the African plains. As a result, an individual woodland caribou can occupy a range of ten thousand square kilometres, which results in naturally low population densities. This causes no problems for the species' survival until their preferred mature forest habitat is altered by logging, mining, road-building, or, more broadly, by the forest-type changes imposed by global warming. All of these changes make landscapes more suitable to moose and deer. As populations of these "generalist" species increase, so do the numbers of predators like wolves, further impacting caribou populations. What's more, the wispy old man's beard lichen that forms the bulk of the caribou diet only grows in mature boreal forest and is slow to regenerate after logging, and roads increase wolves' mobility. And white-tailed deer carry a parasitic brain worm that's 100 percent lethal in woodland caribou. The gist of the theory is, according to Pukaskwa ecologist John Haselmayer, "What's good for moose and deer is bad for caribou. And for many years, land management policies have been geared toward increasing moose and deer numbers."

At the same time, woodland caribou biology isn't resilient to rapid changes to the landscape. Females start to reproduce around the age of two and a half and will bear at most one calf per year. One estimate pegs yearling calf mortality at 50 to 80 percent. Best scientists can tell, this low-density approach to rearing offspring is a means of keeping predator populations in check and is enough to survive in the right habitat, explains Justina Ray, the executive director of the Wildlife Conservation Society of Canada, a Toronto-based non-profit where she also serves as a senior scientist. But, Ray explains, if environmental conditions change, this life history makes it hard for them to keep up if the population starts declining.

Climate change could be a death sentence for the species. Drier summers and more fires could easily burn up woodland caribou habitat, while warmer winters and more freezing rain might encase key lichen-rich foraging areas under a veneer of ice, rendering them inaccessible and resulting in starvation. Woodland caribou are currently protected as a priority species in Ontario's 2007 Endangered Species Act (ESA), which has imposed significant protection measures on current and historical habitat and initiated a province-wide recovery plan. But there are significant concerns of how well such legislation will stand up. Northern communities have been quick to wrongly attribute job losses due to a global economic meltdown and a general decrease in demand for Canadian forest products to government policies protecting caribou habitat. In the case of the federal government's boreal (woodland) caribou recovery strategy, the Ottawa-based non-profit Canadian Parks and Wilderness Society gave the species a 60 percent chance of long-term survival as a result of the compromise-based approach of Prime Minister Stephen Harper's regime.

Biologists like Ray put even less faith in legislation holding up in the mineral-rich "Ring of Fire" region of northwestern Ontario, an immense wilderness area in the James Bay Lowlands five hundred kilometres north of Thunder Bay that comprises the province's last woodland caribou stronghold. With an economic windfall and the plight of an endangered species hanging in the balance, Ray is concerned that decision-makers will choose in favour of massive-scale development. "That's the last frontier," says Ray. "Once we destroy it, we won't have much to fall back on."

There are several theories to explain why remnant populations of woodland caribou have persisted along the Lake Superior coastline while the rest of Ontario's population has retreated northward like a stage curtain. First off, protected areas like Pukaskwa National Park, Lake Superior Provincial Park, and Neys Provincial Park safeguard much of the coastal corridor, rendering it off limits to development. Logging hasn't occurred in these areas in decades, allowing a mature, lichen-rich forest to flourish. Then there's the microclimatic effect of Lake Superior, which creates a band of low snowfall area immediately along the shoreline and an area of lake-effect snow farther inland. This

The rugged coastline of Lake Superior receives less snow than inland areas, providing travel corridors for woodland caribou. Meanwhile, interior snowbelts impede wolves' access to the coastline, lessening the risk of predation. These dynamics change when roads improve the wolves' mobility.

effectively provides woodland caribou with a safe haven for most of the year: The deep snow a few kilometres from the coast acts like a moat to keep wolves out; and offshore islands afford refuge for strong-swimming caribou in the summer months, particularly during calving season.

However, as the balance of the caribou range has retreated, the protected habitats on the Lake Superior coast have essentially become islands themselves: A swath of roads and clear-cuts abutting park boundaries separates the parks' herds from the rest of the Ontario's woodland caribou, which persist in viable numbers in many areas north of fifty degrees latitude. While this is fine and well in the short term, the so-called "island effect" imposes strains on the genetic diversity of small, disjunctive populations by increasing the risk of inbreeding. "What we have here is a remnant herd," says Allen. "Although Pukaskwa's small caribou population has persisted for many years, federal and provincial biologists predict it might be too small to sustain itself for many more."

According to the MNR's recovery strategy report on woodland caribou, which was filed in 2008 under the auspices of the ESA, the only way to save the Lake Superior population in the long term is to connect it to northern herds by way of corridors of undisturbed wilderness. Currently, Parks Canada ecologists, MNR biologists, and area stakeholders are investigating the option of reintroducing more caribou to Pukaskwa's boreal forest. But this approach has had little success elsewhere. Few of the thirty-five caribou transported from northern Lake Superior's Slate Islands to Lake Superior Provincial Park in 1989 managed to survive. And of the province's three other reintroduction attempts, only the 1982 transfer of eight caribou to predator-free Michipicoten Island has been successful in the long term (the island is now home to about two hundred caribou).

Ray likens the conservation of biological diversity to health care: We need to choose between an approach involving cautious, informed decision-making, ongoing screening, and regular checkups versus major surgery to repair the effects of long-term neglect. "Often we don't show the necessary restraint and we get in a pickle where all that's left is a very intensive management approach," she says. As a result, places like Pukaskwa may have no other option than to rely on low-success measures like reintroductions, which might be the only way to buy the species more time on Lake Superior's north shore while more restrictive resource development regulations brings new habitat "online" in nearby areas. "We have an opportunity to increase number of caribou in the park while learning more about their movements, preferred habitats, and interactions with wolves and moose," says Allen. "We want to do everything possible to protect this species for generations to come."

The results of Pukaskwa's infrared survey provided a new degree of hope: Whereas helicopter surveys suggested that only four or five woodland caribou remained in the park's backcountry, the heat-sensing cameras indicated a population of sixteen. Despite the surprise jump in park caribou numbers, Allen says the woodland caribou on Lake Superior's north shore are "critically imperiled."

Now, park managers are faced with the equally challenging social and economic aspects of wildlife conservation in the age of the Anthropocene. In both practical and ecological terms, costly, labour-intensive research like that being conducted in Pukaskwa begs the question, *why bother?* There are many things going against the recovery of the park's woodland caribou population, including ongoing development in neighbouring terrain, in addition to the genetic concerns relating to the long-term viability of small populations. At the same time, says Ray, the tax-paying public has been lulled into a "new normal" where decreasing environmental awareness — another symptom of the Anthropocene and so-called condition of "nature deficit disorder" — is dominant among an increasingly urban population. The result is a general lack of concern for environmental issues. "It's not that all species will disappear altogether but their abundances are going down," she notes. "But the average person isn't noticing these changes. It's hard to keep track of that stuff and your baseline slides."

This is why Ray insists that conservation work is essential, if only for what the presence of "indicator" species like woodland caribou reveal about the integrity of the life-supporting functions of the greater environment. "If you've got caribou you've probably got a lot of other stuff," says Ray. This includes other sensitive wildlife ranging from wolverines to warblers, dynamic aquatic habitats, and clean water, not to mention a healthy, intact boreal forest ecosystem essential in regulating the planet's climate by drawing and storing millions of tonnes of atmospheric carbon dioxide. "It's a pretty good assumption to say that if you do right by caribou, you do right by a great number of critical processes," she says. "That's why I spend so much time on this animal."

CHAPTER 15

Across the Snow on Wooden Wings

Most of my early memories of growing up in the rural community of Goulais River, just north of Sault Ste. Marie, involve winter. Back in the early 1980s, we seemed to receive more frequent dumps of snow — usually enough to allow my father to craft a wild bobsleigh course with elaborate banked corners on the bluff behind our house that descended to the river by Christmastime. I remember building a jump at the base of one such run and talking my dad into joining me for a run on my GT Snow Racer sled. But first I had to promise him that I would swerve to miss the jump. I agreed, and we loaded up — my thirty-something father conceding the steering controls to his four-year-old son. Sure enough, I set us on a fast, straight-line course — directly at the jump.

For a brief moment we hung suspended in the air and then crashed to the ground spectacularly. Upon landing, the sled luckily flew in one direction and we careened off in the other. I remember laying on the ice-covered river at the base of the hill with my father for a long while afterwards, staring at the starry sky and feeling guilty for tricking him into the kamikaze run.

Skiing always played an important part of the winters of my early childhood. My first pair of cross-country skis was constructed of wood and built by local Scandinavian craftsmen in my hometown. For a couple of decades, Sault Ste. Marie was home to North America's only manufacturer of wooden cross-country skis, attesting to the region's large number of Nordic immigrants and rich ski culture. Of course, this tradition was lost on my young mind. The skis of my childhood have disappeared, and it wasn't until later, when I became a cross-country enthusiast in my twenties, that I realized the significance of the local ski scene. I learned that some friends had once worked in the ski-building shop, and that the owner of this business, Mauri Luomeranta, was the grandfather of another friend. I became passionate about wooden skis just in time, as it seems like in recent years they've become harder and harder to find.

• • •

In recent years, Enn Poldmaa's threats to burn pieces of cross-country ski heirlooms have become more serious. A series of warm winters in the snow-belt region north of Lake Superior, where Poldmaa and his partner, Robin MacIntyre, run a bed and breakfast and backcountry ski area, has brought Poldmaa to the brink of trying anything — including pagan ceremonies — to bring back the snow. On the wall in Poldmaa and MacIntyre's Goulais River home is a sign paying homage to Heiki Lunta — Hank Snow — one of several Scandinavian gods of winter. It reads, "Let it snow/Let it blow/Let my skis be in controw." Apparently, sacrificing old pairs of wooden skis in a hot bonfire is a means of appeasing Heiki Lunta and Ullr, the famed Norse snow god.

But for Poldmaa, the consequences of warmer winters don't yet equate with the moral impacts of incinerating pieces of cross-country ski heritage. In the 1970s, Poldmaa worked at Canada's only wooden ski factory in his hometown of Sault Ste. Marie, Ontario, thirty kilometres south of where he now operates the Bellevue Valley Bed and Breakfast. So far, Poldmaa and MacIntyre have remained amongst the ranks of respectful collectors of wooden skis. But each year as the weather warms and the winters come later and later, the thought of sacrifice takes on a greater meaning.

When Mauri Luomeranta first came to Canada, he arrived as a traveller, not an immigrant. Luomeranta was seeking adventure, and ended up finding a new life direction. The twenty-five-year-old native of Vaasa, Finland, planned to spend five years exploring Canada and then return to Scandinavia to settle down in his homeland. In 1958, Luomeranta arrived in Sault Ste. Marie, Ontario, a city of seventy-five thousand that's located in the heart of the Great Lakes and at the eastern edge of a Scandinavian stronghold surrounding Lake Superior.

It didn't take long for Luomeranta to become a central figure in the area's burgeoning cross-country ski scene. A former competitive racer, he found a community of similarly skilled skiers. Finnish ex-pats started Sault Ste. Marie's cross-country ski club in 1953. The early ski races must've been some-thing to see: Competitive experts going head to head in deep snow, following sinuous courses through the trees and bombing down the powdery hills. The frontrunners of such races would've faced the double challenge of warding off competitors' advances and breaking trail. After several years of this sort of off-trail skiing, the group began cutting trails in the hardwood and white pine forest of the Hiawatha Highlands, just north of the city, in 1960.

For new immigrants, the Finnish club was an asylum that took the edge off of the acclimatization process. Luomeranta's early days in Canada were dominated by a full schedule of social activities, including skiing and dinners and dances organized by the club. He learned to speak English as fast as he came to decide he would stay in Canada, and used his machinist trade to find work in a Sault Ste. Marie foundry.

It goes without saying that cross-country skiing was a focal point for the local Finnish community. About the same time as the Sault Finnish Ski Club was formed, Uuno Rastas, a former competitor on the national Finn ski team, became Canada's first commercial ski manufacturer, albeit at a decidedly small scale. Since good skis were hard to come by without paying expensive import duties, Rastas supplied the community with "Sault Ste. Marie Special" wooden skis he fashioned by hand in his basement.

Luomeranta served as the president of the Sault Finnish Ski Club for nearly a decade. In the early 1970s, Rastas invited him to help out with his wooden ski business, which by then had ramped up production and had expanded from Rastas's basement to a barn on the outskirts of the city. Still, Luomeranta says the construction process was painfully slow. Each ski was shaped by hand with minimal technology. At best, a half-dozen workers could make twenty pairs of skis per day, explains Luomeranta, who now lives just east of Sault Ste. Marie, where he maintains his own network of trails. "Rastas had a lot of experience as a carpenter and was a fantastic skier, but he knew nothing about mass production," says Luomeranta. "From my work as a tradesman, I knew how to make a product as efficiently as possible."

Luomeranta and Rastas purchased a new, industrial-size production facility in 1973. Together, they made "a few thousand" pairs of skis. But Luomeranta quickly became tired of Rastas's tedious manufacturing process and pulled out of the partnership. In 1975, the production of Rastas skis ceased and Luomeranta investigated the idea of taking over. A year later, he found a national distributor based in Toronto who was interested in purchasing wooden skis in bulk. It didn't take long for the machinist Luomeranta to dial in a more streamlined manufacturing process. At peak production he employed twenty-two workers, including a young Enn Poldmaa, and turned out an impressive

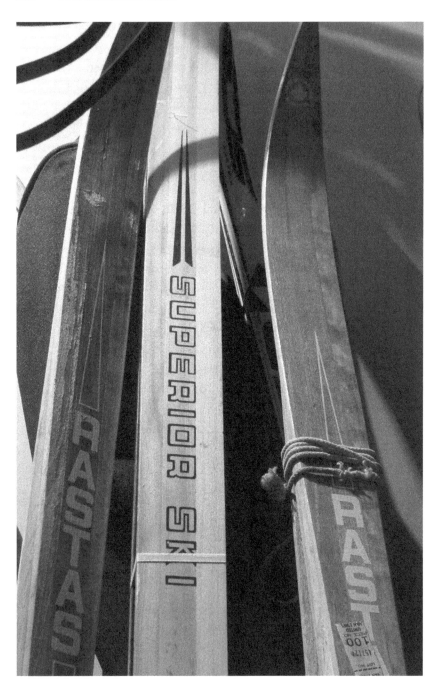

Two generations of Sault Ste. Marie–built cross-country skis: The original wooden skis built by Finnish Canadian Uuno Rastas in the 1960s and Mauri Luomeranta's Superior Ski, which were mass-produced in the 1970s.

160 pairs of skis a day using a series of mechanized planers, laminators, and clamps — most of his own design. His generation of wooden skis was stamped with the "Superior Ski" brand.

Luomeranta's legend among Sault Ste. Marie skiers grew. According to one story, the research and development phase of Superior Skis involved Luomeranta towing children behind the family station wagon on suburban streets to test the durability of various base laminations. He tried to employ local woods as much as possible, using Ontario birch for the base of the ski and local pine for the topsheet; he only imported harder, more impact- and abrasion-resistant hickory to use for the edges. His skis were primarily designed for the beginners that flooded the North American cross-country ski market in the 1970s. By sourcing materials locally, Luomeranta was able to keep costs relatively low. Prices for Superior Skis ranged from $35 to $50, compared to $60 for imported skis from Scandinavia. In their heyday, Luomeranta estimates that fifteen hundred pairs of Superior Skis were sold annually in Sault Ste. Marie alone. On the growing network of groomed cross-country ski trails in Sault Ste. Marie, Superior Skis were king.

There's something sacred about wooden cross-country skis — especially if they were crafted by hand in your hometown. Each fall, I fill my house with the pungent scent of pine tar as I bathe the honey-brown bases of my vintage Rastas skis. Torching the bases bubbles and burns the tar; and rubbing the last of the hot tar with a rag into the skis leaves them rich, smooth, and chocolaty brown. Compared to ironing in toxic fluoro-based waxes into modern plastic, fibreglass, and carbon-fibre skis, the old-school process is decided organic and comforting.

It must be admitted that the earlier generation Rastas skis were far more aesthetically pleasing than Luomeranta's Superior Skis. Mine have a shapely hourglass sidecut with a narrow waist and moderately wide tip, or "shovel" — perfect for skiing softer, ungroomed trails in the traditional style. The binding plate underneath the skier's foot tapers from base to topsheet in an attractive hand-carved curve. The tips and tails are wafer-thin and the camber, that is the C-shape curve of a cross-country ski that gives it springy kick and glide, is lively.

Luomeranta says he altered Rastas's design to a more utilitarian shape that was easier to produce in bulk. A series of production line steps laminated twelve pieces of wood to form skis with a decidedly boxy, novice-friendly shape. They still have the warmth of wood, but lack the sensuous curves that could only be produced in the labourious, handcrafted construction of Rastas's skis.

Rastas's and Luomeranta's ski-building ushered in a tradition that was well established in Europe. On his website, *www.woodenskis.com*, ski historian Greg Fengel lists thirty-seven European manufacturers of wooden cross-country skis. Over a century ago, Fengel says three builders emerged for a brief spell in St. Paul, Minnesota, making it "the North American capital of wooden ski production." In 1879, the Strand Ski Company began supplying skis to the early Nordic skiing clubs of Ishpeming, Michigan, and Red Wing, Minnesota. The Northland and Gregg ski companies followed suit, building one-piece skis modelled after Norwegian designs. Well before Rastas became Canada's first ski builder, American production had petered out in favour of importing skis from European manufacturers.

In freshly fallen snow, wooden skis whisper sweet nothings to the trees and feel more lively than those made of less natural materials. I was part of the last generation of youngsters to learn to kick and glide on wooden skis, booting around on the hilly driveway at my grandparents' home in the rural community of Goulais River, just north of Sault Ste. Marie. While I quickly graduated to fibreglass, foam, and eventually carbon-fibre and other high-tech plastics, I have recently got in the habit of using wooden skis for touring in untracked snow. In the right snow conditions — particularly on colder days — wooden skis have superior grip on the uphill section as well as reasonable glide.

When it comes to outdoor gear, I'm a bit of a pack rat. With each ski swap I visit, my quiver of wooden skis grows. Every once in a while, I stumble upon a treasure, like a pair of $5 Norwegian-made touring skis that I discovered in immaculate shape. A good friend of mine has a perfect pair of Superior Skis mounted on his basement wall. But for the most part, the odd remaining pairs of Rastas and Superior Skis have long since lived out their usable life. I suspect that the time will soon come when most of my collection of cracked, camber-less, and rotting wooden skis will eventually go up in flames in ceremonies to appease Heiki Lunta in hopes of blessings of snow.

• • •

Luomeranta entered the ski-building world at a time when popular interest in cross-country skiing was skyrocketing. Suddenly, wool sweaters, duck-billed leather boots, and knee-high socks were a fashionable way to stay in shape during the long months of winter. American cross-country skier Bill Koch's silver in the 1976 Winter Olympics (still the United States' only medal in Nordic skiing) had a lot to do with it, ushering legions of beginners into the sport. The spike in popularity observed in the U.S. was mirrored in Canada, in part due to Pierre Harvey's modest success in the 1984 and 1988 Olympic Games. The invention of freestyle or "skate" skiing happened about the same time, reflecting the surging interest in the sport. The diehard members of the Sault Finnish club were soon forced to share their trails at Hiawatha with others. "It seemed like the number of skiers doubled each year in the seventies," says Luomeranta, who sold his skis at a local shop and at stores across Canada. "It was a good time to be in the cross-country ski business. The trails were full of people."

Ironically, it was this cross-country skiing boom that marked the end of the line for wooden cross-country ski manufacturers around the world. As the sport surged in popularity in the late-1970s, business was brisk for Superior Skis. But so was the call for more durable, maintenance-free skis that didn't require regular treatment with pine tar and blowtorches.

After building over ten thousand pairs of wooden skis, Luomeranta admits that his product was rightfully ousted by synthetics in the early 1980s. He briefly explored the idea of manufacturing skis from plastics, but decided against it and gave up his business in 1981. Three decades later, he still says, with a certain degree of wistful regret, "We just couldn't compete with mass produced foam and fiberglass skis."

Today, Rastas and Superior Skis have become as scarce on Sault Ste. Marie ski trails as the long, cold winters that once buried the area in metre upon metre of snow. As my collection of wooden skis continues to grow, I can't help but imagine the memories held in their parched and rickety bases. Like Poldmaa, I've wondered if fire is the only way to call on superstition to return to times of "real winter." Then I think that the tarring and torching process might be close enough, that maybe Heiki Lunta misses the soft, sensuous *whishhh* of wooden skis in untracked snow.

CHAPTER 16

The New Trading Posts

I remember my first visit to Agawa Crafts, Gerry and June Demers's bustling gift shop in Pancake Bay, north of Sault Ste. Marie. I was seven years old and desperately wanted a Davy Crockett raccoon fur cap. It was the mid-1980s, the heyday of the tourist trade on the Trans-Canada Highway, when roadside restaurants and motels were brimming with motorists making pilgrimages across the country. As always, the Demerses' establishment at Pancake Bay was busier than most. I remember the crowded aisles of Agawa Indian Crafts, where we jostled for position to find my fur hat. I couldn't believe my luck when my parents agreed to buy me one.

Twenty-five years later, the Demerses' business is about the only retail operation remaining on the stretch of highway between Sault Ste. Marie and Wawa. Others have come and gone. I've watched the old gas station and restaurant at Agawa Bay, at the south end of Lake Superior Provincial Park, morph into a junkyard of scrapped automobiles and bundles of spent tires, its buildings partially burned by a suspicious fire. The dozens of small, family-owned motels and restaurants that once graced the highway have been reduced to a mere handful, most having had a revolving door of owners who couldn't get away fast enough. The highway shoulders are littered with realty signs standing in the tall, swaying grasses of abandoned properties, and dreams.

It's telling that one of the other successful businesses along this stretch of high-way has direct ties to the Demers empire: Frank O'Connor and his wife, Gail, worked for Gerry and June in the early 1980s and have applied the same tireless approach to sales and marketing in turning a derelict property at Batchawana Bay into the Voyageurs Lodge and Cookhouse, a friendly, welcoming establishment just north of Sault Ste. Marie that celebrates the rich, colourful history of the Canadian fur trade.

I always got the sense that there was more to Gerry Demers than the tall, muscled and tanned man with a booming voice who greeted people at the Esso gas pumps in Pancake Bay. When I took the time to ask him about his passion for entrepreneurship, I learned about a driven, passionate individual who has inspired hundreds of youth and has the legacy, as O'Connor says, of "sharing Canada with the world."

You can't help but notice the big Agawa Crafts billboard at the top of the Mile Hill on the Trans-Canada Highway, just north of Sault Ste. Marie. It's the first in a parade of roadside placards advertising fishing and hunting licences, beer and liquor sales, a convenience store, gas station, rest area, and high-end craft shop. The signs draw motorists north, counting down the kilometres to Gerry and June Demers's empire at Pancake Bay. They intensify as you approach the small cottage community on Lake Superior about eighty kilometres north of Sault Ste. Marie.

Here, the highway descends from a swampy plateau, crosses the meandering, tannin-coloured Pancake River and runs arrow-straight along the flattened sand dunes where the fur-trading voyageur canoemen of two hundred years ago pulled ashore and used the last of their flour to fry up a batch of flapjacks before re-provisioning at the trading post in Sault Ste. Marie. On the east side of the highway, the bustling parking lot, oversized flags, and non-stop country music of Agawa Crafts and The Canadian Carver is incongruous with the stately red pines and Caribbean-like white sand beach abutting Lake Superior on the other.

There used to be a handful of competing restaurants and gas stations here, but not anymore. That's largely because of the business acumen and indefatigable work ethic of Gerry Demers, the tall, slim, and broad-shouldered man who's most likely the first person you'll meet when you pull into the gas station parking lot. At sixty-five years old, Gerry is a ball of energy. Part drill sergeant, part Walmart greeter, he barks orders to his sheepish staff that's comprised mostly of teenagers and leads them in bounding from car to car, jovially greeting visitors and announcing the availability of free coffee inside, jockeying the gas pumps and squeegeeing windows tirelessly. At first, you might wonder about the man's role in the business' pecking order. He clearly isn't afraid of working the trenches — even the menial tasks of cleaning toilets and mopping floors is part of his job description, responsibilities he shares with the crew of summer students he pays minimum wage. Moreover, there's little doubt the man was up before you this morning (he's on the job at six a.m. every day) and will be wrapping up yet another sixteen-hour day long after you've pulled over for the night at a roadside campground or motel.

The Pancake Bay establishment belonging to Gerry and his wife, June, is a reasonable facsimile of the Hudson's Bay and North West Company trading posts that once dotted Lake Superior's north shore, with a modern-day twist: cars, trucks, and bus-sized recreational vehicles have replaced the canoes and snowshoes of old. Adjacent to the gas pumps, Agawa Crafts is housed in a long, wood-panelled structure with an expansive verandah that's peppered with racks of T-shirts and wool blankets. Inside, the building is packed to the brim with more clothing, books, Canadian jams and maple syrup, trinkets and other odds and ends. Farther back and to the side is The Canadian Carver, a similarly sized square-timbered building with stout, axe-handled wooden doors, where the Demerses showcase the wood carvings and crafts they procure from French Canadian and First Nations artisans from across eastern Canada. The Camper's Store abuts the Carver at right angles. It's the place you go for ice cream, groceries, and beverages of the soft and hard varieties.

When Gerry and June Demers moved to Pancake Bay from Montreal River in 1987, they loaded their gift shops aboard flatbed trailers and hauled them forty kilometres south on the Trans-Canada Highway.

On busy days, traffic usually spills over into the large gravel parking lot next door, where you'd be hard pressed to notice the creek that flows lazily through the north end of the property, obscured by the surrounding fanfare. In behind the bustling complex is terra incognita — an array of trailers and storage sheds plastered with bold-lettered signs reading PRIVATE PROPERTY and YOU HAVE BEEN WARNED. A kennel load of dogs yaps in the background, while crimson and orange pickup trucks emblazoned with *Mishepeshu*, the great horned lynx of the Ojibwa that's depicted in red ochre on the cliffs of nearby Agawa Bay, buzz to and from the backyard abyss.

Paradoxically, as much as this place has the air of a classic tourist trap, it is, for the most part, the real deal. What's more, it's virtually the only remaining retail outlet on the 230-kilometre-long highway between Sault Ste. Marie and Wawa, which has become a veritable graveyard for the tourist trade. The Demerses are passionate about selling fine, authentic, Canadian-made wood carvings and crafts. True, you'll still find the usual assortment of tacky sweatshirts, disposable beach toys, plastic tomahawks, and other kitsch in the back aisles of Agawa Crafts, but mostly you will catch a glimpse of an old, fast-fading Canadian way of life: Freshly smoked Lake Superior trout, braids of sacred sweetgrass picked by Aboriginal hands in southern Ontario, and intricate porcupine-quill baskets handmade on the east coast.

Taken as a whole, the scene bears some resemblance to an anthill, with Gerry and his red-shirted instructional staff moving about at a frenetic pace, maintaining the facilities and serving customers with military efficiency. But if you can catch him for a moment, Gerry will slow down and tell you the story of how the empire came to be. I'd stopped at the place hundreds of times over the summers of my youth and young adulthood, making hasty arrangements with the Demerses to hawk sea-kayak day tours and instructional courses to walleyed tourists from an ad hoc sales booth set up haphazardly in his parking lot, grabbing a free cup of tea for the road, or nursing an ice cream cone on a bench and observing the peculiarities of the passing throng. Then I finally took the time to get to know the man on a humid and drizzly mid-August morning.

"So, how much longer are you going to keep running this place?" hollers a customer across racks of moccasins in Agawa Crafts, stealing one of my interview questions.

"About another hundred years," laughs Gerry, leaving me by the book-shelves and jam sample station near the back of the store to chat with his customer, clearly one of the many acquaintances he has made in forty years as an entrepreneur. He's stopped another two times by staff and customers before he finally leads me into a maze of cubicles at the back of the store. His desk is bare, except for a notepad and pen. I get the impression that it's a place he rarely frequents.

"You'll notice that there's no computer," Gerry says, as if following my gaze has enabled him to read my mind. "I don't Twitter, I don't blog. To me, Skype sounds like a kind of bird you see on the beach. We have a website and email and all that stuff, but I have nothing to do with those parts of the business. I just want to be outside, serving the motoring public."

He might have picked up this initiative from his father, a salesman who moved the Demers family from Brantford, Ontario, north to Sault Ste. Marie when Gerry was nine years old. Gerry returned to southern Ontario to study economics, business administration, and sociology at Hamilton's McMaster University, but his heart was always on the north shore of Lake Superior. He worked a few years for the Toronto Dominion bank before his patience ran thin. "King and Bay had no allure to me," he says. "I wasn't interested in working for a large corporation and I didn't like the type of environment in southern Ontario. I missed fishing and hunting. I missed the North."

Customer service was at the top of Gerry's business plan in 1971, when he heard about a Gulf Oil station that had come up for lease in Montreal River Harbour, a hamlet nestled between Lake Superior and the Trans-Canada Highway, 120 kilometres north of Sault Ste. Marie. He acquired the lease and moved north. Along with the gas station he established a gift shop with a tiny four-by-ten-foot showroom. With a $1,000 loan and his trademark do-anything enthusiasm, he "decided to start a business and see where it goes."

The job was by no means glamorous. Once, "I had to hand bail the septic tank one bucket at a time," he says. "You quickly realize that it's not a white-shirt-and-tie kind of job." But the early days established the selfless and tire-less work ethic that's been at the heart of his success. "You're pretty well chief, cook, and bottle-washer. You're the buyer, the seller, and the one responsi-ble for maintaining the buildings," he says. "You work long hours and you're always tired. You quickly realize that they didn't teach you plumbing, electrical, and carpentry work at university, but when you're starting a small business with no money, you learn these skills yourself. You take it one step at a time."

After his first summer as an entrepreneur, he was forced to work for Gulf Oil driving a fuel oil delivery truck to cover the last of his start-up bills. It was a gruelling, messy job that involved long hours on call, driving a massive, ornery fuel truck, and hauling the "seventy-five-foot python," a heavy, pressurized hose that often belched its contents prematurely all over its operator, through snowbanks to fill household oil tanks. At the end of the day, "my landlady wouldn't let me come in the house with any clothes on," he says. The pay was brutal and the hours were insane. "It was the only job I ever quit," he adds with a chuckle.

After the delivery job, Gerry returned to Montreal River with a new incentive to grow his business. The evolution began on a stormy winter day when he met someone who would be critical to the plan. Manitoulin Island native June Middleton was driving home from a visit with her sister in Thunder Bay when she hit a patch of ice and slid off the highway, right outside Gerry's gas station. He came to her aid and set about courting her to move north. Gerry insists that it wasn't until June got involved that the business truly became successful. The couple got married and had their first child, Linette, in 1975. Laura was born in 1977 and Robert in 1980.

After the fuel oil fiasco, he began dedicating the winter months to procuring inventory for his gift shop, which he housed in a new six-hundred-square-foot showroom. In December, Gerry would drive south, visiting First Nations craftspeople in places like Wikwemikong, a reserve on Manitoulin Island, and the various Six Nations reserves of southern Ontario. He soon expanded his road show to Quebec's Lower North Shore and the Maritime provinces to do business with master woodcarvers. Orders were placed in December and pickups were scheduled for March. The challenge then was to fit all the products into his two-ton box van. "It was about the size of a small [delivery] van," he says. "Snow would come through the doors. It was a real gypsy scene."

He soon added neighbouring Texaco and Esso gas stations to his holdings at Montreal River, along with associated gift shops — Agawa Indian Crafts and The Canadian Carver. At one point, Gerry and June employed sixty-five people in the high season. As always, Gerry was the face of the operations and the hardest worker on the site. In 1973, he told Montreal River historian Don Steer, "I do a lot of running on the gasoline pumps. I wore right through the soles of two pairs of Greb boots last summer!"

Frank O'Connor sums up the heyday of Gerry and June Demers's business in three words: "It was wild." It's not that Agawa Crafts and The Canadian Carver aren't busy today, but back when the Demerses were running three gas stations in Montreal River, "there were still lineups at the pumps at eleven o'clock at night," says O'Connor, a Sault Ste. Marie native, who, as a teenager, started jockeying gas for Demers in the late 1970s. Gas was cheap and families were in the habit of taking extended road trips across the country, rather than taking shorter, destination-based vacations as is the norm today. On the job, O'Connor's work schedule consisted of seven days on, seven days off. While they were putting in their eighty-hour weeks, staff lived on site in bunkhouses. "It was pretty remote," says O'Connor. "Students arrived for the week of work on the Ontario Northland bus."

A summer working for Gerry has been the first job for generations of Algoma teens. While it's immediately apparent that Gerry drives his staff hard and with military discipline, he also sets a good example by working alongside them. "My employees quickly learn that the business succeeds because of them, not in spite of them," he says. "I find that many of these kids working their first job will outperform adults." For thirty-five years, the Demerses provided room and board for their staff, but that's changed in the past few years. "Teenagers are full of energy. Even after working for twelve hours, they still had ten hours left for nonsense," he sighs. "I got tired of policing all that. Now I get my rest."

O'Connor remembers the hard work, but also the good times. Some of his best memories are reminiscent of the Wild West. Once, three cows escaped from the back of a cattle truck in Montreal River. Gerry promptly dispatched one in his Texaco lot, and later ended the suffering of the other two when they were found wandering aimlessly along the highway shoulder. "We ate a lot of steaks and roasts that winter," O'Connor recalls. Before the days of commercial delivery services, Gerry says a big part of doing business was running to and from Sault Ste. Marie to pick up supplies. And because "computers weren't invented yet," O'Connor remembers how staff were responsible for filing a pen and paper inventory system that was managed by June.

Laidback Voyageur Lodge and Cookhouse owner Frank O'Connor lacks the tireless bustle of his business mentor, Gerry Demers, but his Highway 17 establishment still fills to capacity on summer weekends.

When Gerry opened his Trapline Trading Post outlet in Pancake Bay, he offered O'Connor the job of managing it. Under Demers's ever-watchful eye, O'Connor oversaw the day-to-day operations of this gift shop on the highway in Pancake Bay from 1981 to 1986. Because he had no time to cook his meals, he got into the habit of eating at Sunny's Gulf gas station across the highway, where he met and fell for his future wife, Gail Gibbs, a local from Batchawana Bay.

As a year-round employee, O'Connor joined Gerry on the winter buying trips. Usually they each piloted their own vehicle, but occasionally they carpooled together. "Gerry would quiz me on marketing strategies and have me analyze different businesses," says O'Connor. "Those were great lessons in entrepreneurship for an impressionable guy in his twenties." When they landed in a First Nation or French Canadian village, O'Connor marvelled at how Demers would integrate into the community. "I was amazed at how well he could hold a conversation in French and how we'd always be taken into people's homes," says O'Connor. "We were in these very Québécois villages and here was this English-speaking dude from Ontario coming to do business and doing it very well. He established relationships with his suppliers and they trusted him." Gerry's approach eliminated intermediaries, explains O'Connor, which enabled him to pay craftspeople fair rates and, in turn, charge his customers more reasonable prices for first-rate goods.

With Gerry's energy dedicated to the "boots to the ground" side of business, June held the fort on the administration end. O'Connor remembers how she pioneered using computer bookkeeping programs to keep record of the empire's massive amount of inventory as soon as they became available in the 1980s. "She's the one who has always kept things tied together," says O'Connor. "It's a great balance."

O'Connor decided to get on with his life in 1986, when he left his managerial role at the Trapline Trading Post and completed an economics degree at Algoma University in Sault Ste. Marie. Then he and Gail moved south to London, Ontario, where he attended teacher's college at the University of Western Ontario and began a career as an elementary- and high-school teacher. His favourite subject to teach was entrepreneurship, sharing the lessons he learned from Gerry and June. Each summer, the couple would return to the cottage where they fell in love on Batchawana Bay.

Until one day, they decided they never wanted to drive south again. It was a sunny August day and the O'Connors felt more reluctant than ever to head back to London for the start of the school year. They'd heard that the old Bluewater restaurant and motel, crumbling alongside the Trans-Canada at the north end of Batchawana Bay, was for sale. They jumped on the chance to come home to Lake Superior. "You always feel like a bit of a hypocrite teaching entrepreneurship when you're not an entrepreneur," says O'Connor. "I was always fascinated with Canadian history after hearing the stories from my dad and reading Pierre Berton and Peter C. Newman. Lake Superior and the voyageurs are central to the story of Canada and its economic growth. Americans are always quick to sing their praises. We thought there was an opportunity to do that here with our own history."

The Voyageurs Lodge and Cookhouse opened its doors in 2003, building on the fur-trade motif with a canoemen-inspired menu replete with beans and bannock, the voyageur paintings of Frances Anne Hopkins on the walls, and a twenty-six-foot fibreglass replica of a voyageur canoe in the parking lot. O'Connor admits that the transition to being a small business owner wasn't easy. "We went from a stable income with summers off to an unstable income and working like crazy throughout the summer," he says. "It's been a change in mindset, but watching your idea flourish is always exciting and now we take our vacation in the winter."

You can see the similarities between the O'Connors' operations and that of their mentors fifteen kilometres up the highway. Frank handles the outdoor jobs while Gail forms the "backbone" of the business behind the scenes as the head chef in the kitchen. Good service is a key to their success, a notion that's supported by their six to eight staff. In its first nine years, the business has won several local and regional awards. The Voyageurs Lodge and Cookhouse differs in its services enough not to compete with the Demerses' juggernaut in Pancake Bay. In fact, O'Connor attributes much of his success to his experience working with Gerry. "He taught me to see things that everyone else does, but to see them differently," says O'Connor. "Batchawana Beach sat here idle for a long time. We saw an opportunity in that."

So when *is* Gerry going to give up his business at Pancake Bay? People like Frank O'Connor insist that he hasn't slowed down at all, that he still has the

Frank and Gail O'Connor came back to Batchawana Bay to create the Voyageurs Lodge and Cookhouse, a restaurant and motel north of Sault Ste. Marie.

same energy as when he started forty years ago. In light of economic slow-downs and the simple fact that fewer people are travelling the highway these days, Gerry says he's put even more emphasis on customer service. "We earn trust by delivering value," he notes. Over the years, he's collected more change for the Alzheimer's Society than any other retailer or restaurant in the area, and seeks to correct the social impacts of heightened border secu-rity through ambassadorship. "We're representing the business, Algoma, Ontario, and Canada. We try to fix the negative experiences that people might have had elsewhere in their travels."

In 1987, a year after the O'Connors' departure, the combined effects of slowing traffic and the need to send his oldest daughter Linette to high school encouraged the Demerses to close the gas pumps at Montreal River and load their gift shops onto flatbeds and move them south to their property at Pancake Bay. Now, with a single base located at the very end of the school-bus route to Sault Ste. Marie, the establishment continued to flourish. While road-tripping tourists still constituted a large percentage of business, the Demerses also benefitted from campers at popular Pancake Bay Provincial Park, on the lake side of the highway.

The local rumour mill has implied that Agawa Crafts, The Canadian Carver, and the Campers Store have been for sale informally for several years. When I ask him about it, Demers reluctantly admits, "After forty years it's time for us to look at retirement and get on with the rest of our lives. I really want to travel to some of the places in Canada that my customers tell me about." For June, a relationship with an orphaned German shepherd dog evolved into becoming one of North America's top breeders of Belgian schipperkes, knee-high dogs with flowing jet-black fur and an intense sense of loyalty to their human companions. She also breeds Alaskan klee kai dogs, rare, miniature husky-like dogs.

O'Connor wonders if there's anyone amongst the current generation of entrepreneurs with the savvy and energy to come in and take over. "Gerry's from the old school," he says. "You've got to be one hard-working dude to take that over. Most young people think differently. They don't want to work that hard."

In our hour-long conversation, Gerry and I are interrupted several times when employees come to ask their boss for direction. Mostly, it's apparent that he trusts them. It's the end of the summer, and the empire is running as smoothly as ever. In a few weeks, after Labour Day, business will wind down as traffic slows. I imagine it must be a both a letdown and a relief, but Gerry begs to differ. "You don't have time to feel let down," he says. "A change in seasons means it's time for different stuff. We start getting nighttime frosts and the geese start flying south. You start noticing ice on the puddles in the parking lot. The job tasks switch to getting the place ready for winter."

He closes down at the end of October and spends all of November preparing the facilities for winter. Then, in December, he'll be on the road south, in time to arrive on the reserves of southern Ontario's Six Nations by the first Monday of the month, as always. He'll take holidays over Christmas and New Years, tour trade shows in January and February, and then pick up his inventory in March, ready to open up shop for another season. When he finally calls it quits, will he miss it?

"I'm sure I will," he says. "Mostly it's the people. My suppliers are my friends. And my customers — so many of them come from the big city and when they get here you can see their demeanour changes, the facade comes off and they slow down. I'll miss the blue sky days, the first snow, and the little kids.

"But when it's time to get out, it's time to get out. Some people like to think that they're building a monument to their life," he continues. "On this highway, nothing is permanent. That's an obvious fact. So you do what you can while you're still around."

AFTERWORD

Almost a decade has passed since the late May evening when my friend David Wells and I sat on the sweeping sand and gravel beach facing Lake Superior at the mouth of the Dog River, thirty kilometres west of Wawa, and wondered what this place would be like in fifty years. Would it be covered in Club Med–type hotels and swarming with tourists? Might we be watching the trickling outflow of a massive hydroelectric dam, its turbines whirring under the force of Denison Falls, the 150-foot cataract just upstream? Or could it be developed for cottages, with personal watercrafts and powerboats buzzing offshore? The best option we could come up with is that the place would be deserted, like it was on that spring day.

I'm happy to report that the better part of a decade into our thought experiment, Dog River remains much the same. Spring still arrives with the contours of the beach reshaped by autumn gales and winter ice; you can still scoop drinking water right off the beach; and, if you tune your entire body just right, you can still feel the earth-shaking power of Denison Falls upstream. In fact, I'm even happier to say that there are good odds the place will remain the same for another generation to enjoy because it is now protected by a provincial park.

Meanwhile, back down the coast in Michipicoten, talk of a proposed aggregate quarry that would've blasted shoreline rock and shattered Wells's outfitting business and ecotourism lodge has been silenced by a global economic crisis and, perhaps, the undercurrents of a newfound awareness of the intrinsic role Lake Superior plays in northeastern Ontario's economy — and psyche. It's telling that in the summer of 2011, over a quarter of the population of job-strapped Wawa — some five hundred residents — signed a petition against a multi-year plan to study area bedrock as a deep repository for spent nuclear fuel bundles. Even if the waste dump never came to fruition, the studies alone would've injected millions of dollars into the local economy. But many locals wanted none of it. At the top of their reasons for

The view from the top of Denison Falls on the Dog River. This remote, fifty-metre-tall water-fall located a few kilometres inland from Lake Superior was a favourite of Bill Mason, a famous Canadian canoeist, filmmaker, artist, and author. Mason's efforts to raise awareness of Canada's endangered rivers saved many wild waterways from the threat of hydroelectric development. Though it's contained within a provincial waterway park, Denison Falls is still listed as a potential source of thirty-five-and-a-half megawatts of hydroelectricity by the Ontario Power Authority.

opposing the idea were concerns over the threat of radiation escaping from the so-called "deep geological vaults" and contaminating the big Great Lake on Wawa's doorstep.

There are similar tide shifts up and down the shore. In Marathon, citizens have rallied behind developing a new platinum, copper, and nickel mine with an environmental conscience; Terrace Bay has, for the most part, cleaned up the awful legacy of Kimberly Clark's pulp mill and embraced the image of a clean Lake Superior as a town motto, with two Slate Island woodland caribou emblazoned on its town coat of arms; and down the road in Rossport, Nipigon, and Red Rock, Parks Canada's recently formed Lake Superior National Marine Conservation Area is being heralded as a tourism-based initiative that balances economic benefits with the permanent protection of the region's natural heritage.

Of course, there are always threats. The impacts of climate change are being manifested on Lake Superior's water column and coastline with alarming alacrity. As water temperatures have increased, corresponding changes have been observed in the lakeshore's unique communities of vegetation — wispy and cactus-like glacial throwbacks that have persisted since the last ice age due to the lake's perennially cool waters. But Lake Superior isn't so cold anymore. Botanists are now witnessing these species' demise, as well as the die-off of a unique subspecies of white birch tree that grows old and tall in the wet, fog-drenched hills surrounding Lake Superior.

Herewith a greater awareness is an impetus for action. It was the threat of ecological change that inspired a couple from Minnesota to hike all 2,575 kilometres of Lake Superior's coastline in the summer of 2010. Husband-and-wife naturalists Mike Link and Kate Crowley took photographs every five kilometres along their walk and recorded sightings of rare, at-risk species like woodland caribou and peregrine falcons. They hope that this "baseline data" — as yet never collected for the entire lake — will be useful for measuring changes in the future, and they envisioned their walk as a rallying cry for community action.

"We have a lot of concerns about the future," Link told me in a telephone interview when I asked him to explain the goal of the expedition. "But our message is to encourage people to look around and learn to love the lake, and then they will help take care of it. We can shake fists, but people do what they feel in their hearts."

Having done my own fair share of fist-shaking, I've come to realize that Link is right. It's first-hand experience with a place that develops a sense of compassion for it. The philosopher Keats wrote, "Nothing ever becomes real till it is experienced." Each summer, my wife Kim and I have made a point of taking my little sister, Cameron, on sea-kayak and canoe trips on Lake Superior. In her first trip, at age eleven, my sister marvelled at the size of the bald eagles we saw perched atop the cliffs at the north end of Lake Superior Provincial Park. She laughed back at calling loons and was amazed at the clarity of the water. "Could I touch bottom here?" she repeatedly asked as we glided in sea kayaks over enough crystalline water to bury a three-storey building.

There's an innocence and sense of awe for the natural world in children that we adults would do well to emulate. I think my grandfather recognized this in rallying youngsters to join him in his endless missions in search of Inchcape Rock. Deep in his heart, perhaps, T.J. O'Connor knew that in sharing his love for Lake Superior with his grandchildren he was increasing the odds that it would remain pristine, magical, and awe-inspiring well into the future. Maybe that's the same impetus behind the guided sea-kayak tours my friends David Wells and Mike Petzold offer on Lake Superior: to increase the ranks of those who know, love, and will ultimately stand up to protect this place.

Reading by firelight at day's end on Patterson Island, amidst the Slate Islands archipelago.

During the most recent canoe trip Kim and I took with Cameron along the Lake Superior coast, we swam in a pool beneath a pounding waterfall and paddled on glass-calm water. The mid-June bugs were horrendous in camp, but somehow Cameron, now thirteen years old, seemed to hardly notice. We scrambled on the rocks and while we hiked along the shore I pointed out members of Lake Superior's unique population of Arctic plants. At the end of the trip, she raved about how good food tasted in the wilderness, and chattered excitedly about how she'd finally figured out how to cup her hands over her mouth to replicate a loon's yodelling call. I was most taken aback when we dropped her off at her house. She pulled on my arm, gave me a hug, and told me she loved me. I smiled because I knew what she really meant: she was in love with Lake Superior.

ACKNOWLEDGEMENTS

The best thing about fully immersing yourself in an area are the relationships that come with it. For the past ten years, I've made Lake Superior's north shore my home. Its wild shores, tributary rivers, watershed lakes, and coastal communities are where I endeavour to spend as much time as possible. In my infatuation with this place, I've got to know some wonderful people. My wife Kim and I met while working together as guides at Naturally Superior Adventures on the shore of Michipicoten Bay. In the ensuing years, Kim has joined me on countless adventures and has always provided loving support for my lifestyle as a vagrant writer.

Also in Michipicoten, my stalwart friend David Wells has offered me years of encouragement, employment, and a place to sleep, eat, and paddle — the most important things I know. In the final days of preparing my manuscript, he offered me a desk in his cabin, a small log structure perched on greenstone bedrock with a wall of windows overlooking the lake. It is the most inspiring view in the world.

Thanks to my parents, who shared with me a passion for the creative arts, a sense of curiosity, and always encouraged me to follow my heart. My step-mother, artist Sandra Hodge, kindly volunteered to provide an illustrated map for this book.

Countless friends up and down the north shore have offered me much over the years: Mike and Colleen Petzold of Caribou Expeditions in Goulais River, my surf bud Ray Boucher in Wawa, guiding mentor Tarmo Poldmaa, staunch environmentalists and backcountry skiers Robin MacIntyre and Enn Poldmaa in the Bellevue Valley, Kenny and Shirley Mills in Michipicoten Harbour, and Bruce Lash in Sault Ste. Marie. Master craftsman Torfinn Hansen and his partner, Mary Jo Cullen, were always generous with availing their wonderful cottage whenever I needed a place for an extended stay. Thanks also to Jorma Paloniemi and his partner, Lorraine Wakely, for sharing their tireless and collective sense of all-season adventure.

A few of the stories in this volume were offshoots of work I did for several magazines and newspapers. Tim Shuff, the former editor of *Adventure Kayak* magazine, made great contributions to my early development as a writer and has become a great friend. I have always enjoyed working with Victoria Foote at *ON Nature* magazine. Jeff Moag's sharp editing with *Canoe & Kayak* magazine helped me win a Northern Lights Award for travel journalism. Thanks also to Martin Zibauer and Michelle Kelly at *Cottage Life* for entertaining my ideas from Ontario's frontier. Similarly, Darren and Michelle McChristie have always provided space for my work in producing *Superior Outdoors* magazine from their home in Thunder Bay. Barry Penhale and Jane Gibson, founders of Natural Heritage Books (an imprint of Dundurn), responded to my proposal for a book project with immediate support.

Thanks also to the Ontario Arts Council for financial support through its Writers' Reserve program.

Finally, thanks to all those who stand up for Lake Superior and realize that the joys of its rugged beauty, wild mystique, and sweet-tasting water are both endless and fragile.

RECOMMENDED READING

Chisholm, Barbara, Andrea Gutsche, and Russell Floren. *Superior: Under the Shadow of the Gods,* Toronto: Lynx Images, Toronto, 1999.

Drew, Wayland and Bruce Litteljohn. *Superior: The Haunted Shore.* Toronto: Firefly, 1995.

Drew, Wayland. *Halfway Man.* Toronto: Oberon, 1989.

_____. *The Wabeno Feast.* Toronto: House of Anansi Press, 2001.

Grady, Wayne. *The Great Lakes: The Natural History of a Changing Region.* Vancouver: Greystone, 2007.

McGuffin, Gary and Joanie. *Great Lakes Journey.* Toronto: McClelland & Stewart, 2003.

_____. *Superior: Journeys on an Inland Sea.* Erin Mills, ON: Boston Mills Press, 1995.

Newman, Bill, Sarah Ohmann, and Don Dimond. *Sea Kayaking Lakes Superior and Michigan.* Guilford, CT: Globe Pequot, 1999.

Nute, Grace Lee. *The Voyageur.* St. Paul, MN: Minnesota Historical Society, 1987.

Raffan, James. *Fire in the Bones.* Toronto: HarperCollins, 1996.

Wilkens, Charles. *Breakfast at the Hoito.* Toronto: Natural Heritage, 1997.

Wright, Larry and Patricia. *Great Lakes Lighthouses Encyclopedia.* Erin Mills, ON: Boston Mills Press, 2006.

ABOUT THE AUTHOR

Conor Mihell is an award-winning environmental and adventure travel journalist based in Sault Ste. Marie, Ontario. He is a frequent contributor to *explore*, *Cottage Life*, and the *Globe and Mail*, and is currently an editor-at-large with *Canoe & Kayak* magazine. He is also a long-time sea-kayak and canoe guide on Lake Superior and its inflowing rivers, and an instructor of outdoor adventure leadership for regional outfitters and at Sault College of Applied Arts and Technology. Mihell grew up on Lake Superior's north shore. His family heritage in the region dates back nearly two hundred years and includes a Lake Superior lighthouse keeper, postmaster, and Sault Ste. Marie town clerk. *The Greatest Lake* is his first book. Visit his website at *www.conormihell.com*.

Photo by Aaron Peterson (*www.aaronpeterson.net*).

INDEX

Italicized page numbers refer to image captions.

OF RELATED INTEREST

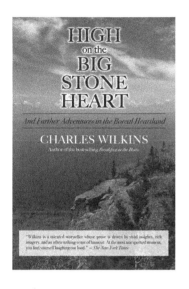

High on the Big Stone Heart
And Further Adventures in the Boreal
Heartland
Charles Wilkins
978-1550028652
$24.99

High on the Big Stone Heart is a collection of vibrant and entertaining essays on the people and places of Canada's Boreal North as seen through the eyes of one of the country's most celebrated writers of non-fiction. Accompany Charles Wilkins as he ranges across the wilds of northern Quebec; ventures deep into the subarctic Yukon in search of caribou; and tracks the north coast of Lake Superior, the world's most elegant and mysterious body of fresh water. Meet Murray Monk, trapper extraordinaire, and Barney Giesler, the king of the wooden boat builders. Trace the route of the Toronto Maple Leafs' Bill Barilko, star of the 1951 Stanley Cup final, on his last and fatal fishing trip to James Bay. Join Maurice "Rocket" Richard on the backwoods adventures that sustained him throughout his troubled career. Follow Wilkins himself as he embarks on a wilderness survival test with nothing but the clothes on his back. This is a book for anyone drawn to the magic of the North, and by the characters who inhabit that epic terrain.

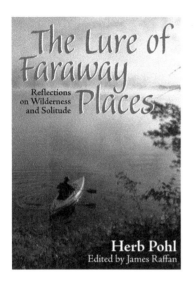